PEARSON

my World

Social Studies™

We Do Our Part

PEARSON

Boston, Massachusetts
Chandler, Arizona
Glenview, Illinois
Upper Saddle River, New Jersey

ISBN-13: 978-0-328-63927-4
ISBN-10: 0-328-63927-3
12 13 14 V011 17 16 15

Program Consulting Authors

The Colonial Williamsburg Foundation
Williamsburg, Virginia

Dr. Linda Bennett
Associate Professor, Department of Learning, Teaching, & Curriculum
College of Education
University of Missouri
Columbia, MO

Dr. Jim Cummins
Professor of Curriculum, Teaching, and Learning
Ontario Institute for Studies in Education
University of Toronto
Toronto, Ontario

Dr. James B. Kracht
Byrne Chair for Student Success
Executive Associate Dean
College of Education and Human Development
College of Education
Texas A&M University
College Station, Texas

Dr. Alfred Tatum
Associate Professor, Director of the UIC Reading Clinic
Literacy, Language, and Culture Program
University of Illinois at Chicago
Chicago, Illinois

Dr. William E. White
Vice President for Productions, Publications and Learning Ventures
The Colonial Williamsburg Foundation
Williamsburg, VA

Consultants and Reviewers

PROGRAM CONSULTANT

Dr. Grant Wiggins
Coauthor, *Understanding by Design*

ACADEMIC REVIEWERS

Bob Sandman
Adjunct Assistant Professor of Business and Economics
Wilmington College–Cincinnati Branches
Blue Ash, OH

Jeanette Menendez
Reading Coach
Doral Academy Elementary
Miami, FL

Kathy T. Glass
Author, *Lesson Design for Differentiated Instruction*
President, Glass Educational Consulting
Woodside, CA

Roberta Logan
African Studies Specialist
Retired, Boston Public Schools/ Mission Hill School
Boston, MA

PROGRAM TEACHER REVIEWERS

Glenda Alford-Atkins
Eglin Elementary School
Eglin AFB, FL

Andrea Baerwald
Boise, ID

Ernest Andrew Brewer
Assistant Professor
Florida Atlantic University
Jupiter, FL

Riley D. Browning
Gilbert Middle School
Gilbert, WV

Charity L. Carr
Stroudsburg Area School District
Stroudsburg, PA

Jane M. Davis
Marion County Public Schools
Ocala, FL

Stacy Ann Figueroa, M.B.A.
Wyndham Lakes Elementary
Orlando, FL

LaBrenica Harris
John Herbert Phillips Academy
Birmingham, AL

Marianne Mack
Union Ridge Elementary
Ridgefield, WA

Emily L. Manigault
Richland School District #2
Columbia, SC

Marybeth A. McGuire
Warwick School Department
Warwick, RI

Laura Pahr
Holmes Elementary
Chicago, IL

Jennifer Palmer
Shady Hills Elementary
Spring Hill, FL

Diana E. Rizo
Miami-Dade County Public Schools/Miami Dade College
Miami, FL

Kyle Roach
Amherst Elementary, Knox County Schools
Knoxville, TN

Eretta Rose
MacMillan Elementary School
Montgomery, AL

Nancy Thornblad
Millard Public Schools
Omaha, NE

Jennifer Transue
Northampton, PA

Megan Zavernik
Howard-Suamico School District
Green Bay, WI

Dennise G. Zobel
Pittsford Schools–Allen Creek
Rochester, NY

Social Studies Handbook

⊙ Reading and Writing

My Community, My Country

THE BIG ? How do people best cooperate?

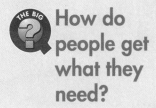

Working to Meet Our Needs

How do people get what they need?

The World Around Us

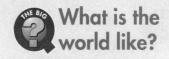
THE BIG ? **What is the world like?**

Celebrating Our Traditions

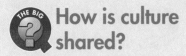 How is culture shared?

Our Nation Past and Present

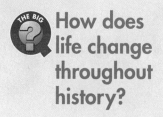
How does life change throughout history?

Draw Conclusions

Use what you already know to help you understand what is happening.

Main Idea and Details

Main Idea
What is the selection all about?

Details

Cause and Effect

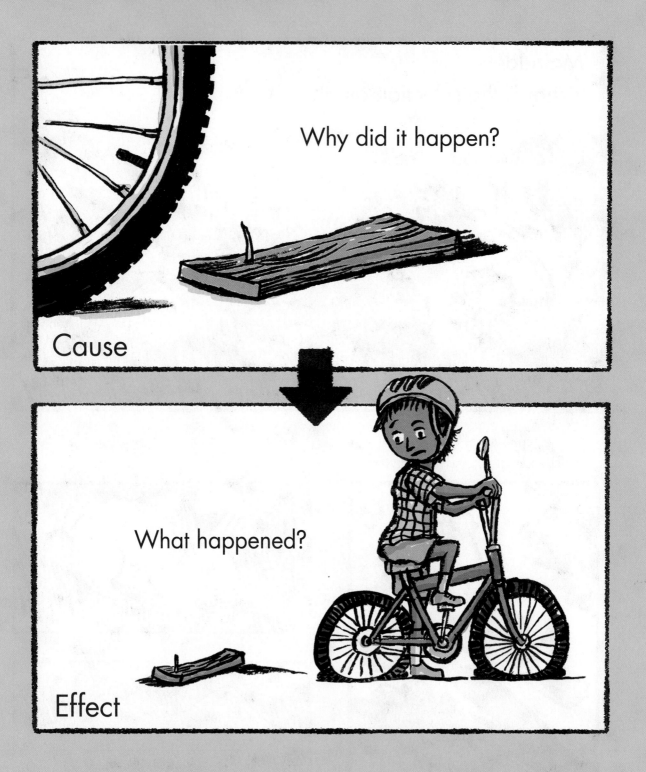

Why did it happen?

Cause

What happened?

Effect

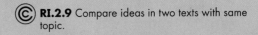
Compare and Contrast

Fact and Opinion

A statement of fact can be proven true or false.

Fact

A statement of opinion tells someone's ideas or feelings.

Opinion

The Writing Process

Good writers follow steps when they write. Here are five steps that will help you become a good writer!

Prewrite	Plan your writing.
Draft	Write your first draft.
Revise	Make your writing better.
Edit	Check your writing.
Share	Share your writing with others.

21st Century Learning Online Tutor

You can go online to myworldsocialstudies.com to practice the skills listed below.
These are skills that will be important to you throughout your life.
After you complete each skill tutorial online, check it off here in your worktext.

◉ Target Reading Skills

- [ ] Main Idea and Details
- [ ] Cause and Effect
- [ ] Classify and Categorize
- [ ] Fact and Opinion
- [ ] Draw Conclusions
- [ ] Generalize
- [ ] Compare and Contrast
- [ ] Sequence
- [ ] Summarize

Collaboration and Creativity Skills

- [ ] Solve Problems
- [ ] Work in Cooperative Teams
- [ ] Resolve Conflict
- [ ] Generate New Ideas

Graph Skills

- [ ] Interpret Graphs
- [ ] Create Charts
- [ ] Interpret Timelines

Map Skills

- [ ] Use Longitude and Latitude
- [ ] Interpret Physical Maps
- [ ] Interpret Economic Data on Maps
- [ ] Interpret Cultural Data on Maps

Critical Thinking Skills

- [ ] Compare Viewpoints
- [ ] Use Primary and Secondary Sources
- [ ] Identify Bias
- [ ] Make Decisions
- [ ] Predict Consequences

Media and Technology Skills

- [ ] Conduct Research
- [ ] Use the Internet Safely
- [ ] Analyze Images
- [ ] Evaluate Media Content
- [ ] Deliver an Effective Presentation

My Community, My Country

my Story Spark

How do people best cooperate?

Draw a picture of how you and your classmates cooperate to get a job done.

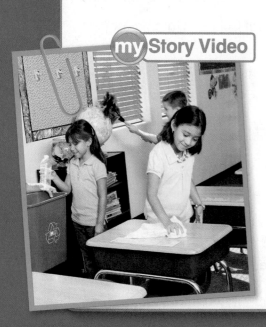

my Story Video

Begin With a Song

Our Country Today

Sing to the tune of "Rockabye, Baby."

When people vote
They each make a choice.
We are all citizens.
We have a voice.

We elect people
To serve and to lead.
With honesty and fairness
In action and deed.

Vocabulary Preview

citizen

respect

responsible

government

rights

Circle examples of these words in the picture.

law

court

Congress

symbol

independence

We Are Good Citizens

Envision It!

Circle examples of people who are taking care of the things around them.

A **community** is a place where people work, live, or play together. Your school is one kind of community. A **citizen** is a member of a community, state, and country.

Ways to Be a Good Citizen

Good citizens care about themselves and others. They listen to one another. They also help one another. A good citizen shows **respect,** or concern for others. When you are fair and honest with others, you are being a good citizen.

1. **Fill in** the blank.

Good citizens are _____

_____

We respect others when we share.

I will know ways to be a good citizen.

Vocabulary

community
citizen
respect
responsible

Good Citizens at School

There are many ways to be a good citizen at school. You can listen to other people's ideas. This shows that you have respect for them. You can share your own ideas. You can also help clean up and take care of school supplies.

You can be a good citizen on the playground, too. Be sure to take turns and be fair when playing. Remember to follow the rules. Rules tell us what to do and what not to do.

2. ◉ **Main Idea and Details**
   Underline two ways you can be a good citizen in school.

Good citizens are fair and take turns.

Citizens in the Community

You are a citizen of your community. Communities can be different sizes. A town is a small community. A city is a big community.

There are many ways you and your family can help in your community. You can help plant trees in a park. You can help clean up a playground.

The people who live near you are part of your neighborhood. They are called neighbors. You can help make your neighborhood a nice place to live. You can pick up trash. You can help a neighbor rake leaves. You can say hello and talk to people you know.

A mural, or painted wall, can make a community more beautiful.

It is important to be a responsible citizen. **Responsible** means taking care of important things. When you clean your room, you are being responsible at home. When you help clean up a park, you are being responsible in your community.

3. **Draw** a picture of how you can help in your community.

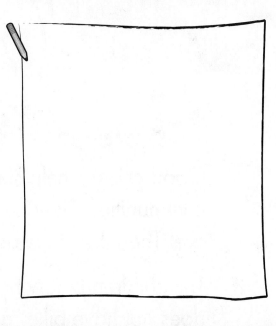

Got it?

4. ◉ **Draw Conclusions** Why is it important to be a good citizen?

_____

_____

5. ❓ **Write** something you and your classmates can do to be responsible citizens.

my Story Ideas

_____

_____

_____

_____

🔲 **Stop!** I need help with _____

▶ **Go!** Now I know _____

Taking Action

Good citizens help solve problems in their communities. They find out what the problems are. Then they take action to solve the problem.

The children below have a problem. Their school does not have bike racks. Here are the steps they took to help solve their problem.

1. Children ride their bikes to school. There is no place to keep the bikes there.

2. Children tell the principal about the problem. She says a bake sale can help raise money.

3. Children raise enough money at the bake sale to buy bike racks.

4. Now the children can keep their bikes at school.

Try it!

1. **Look** at the pictures. **Write** how the children solved their problem.

   _____

   -

   _____

   -

   _____

2. **Draw** a picture of citizens in your community taking action to solve a problem.

Our Rights as Citizens

Envision It!

Look at the pictures.

These people are becoming citizens of the United States of America.

Our country is called the United States of America. People who are born here are citizens of the United States. People who are not born here can apply to become citizens and take an oath of allegiance.

Our Government

A long time ago, our country's leaders wrote a plan for our country. This plan is called the United States Constitution. The Constitution tells us how to run our government. A **government** is a group of people who work together to run a city, a state, or a country. The Constitution tells us how to make laws that keep us safe and help us get along.

1. ⊙ **Draw Conclusions Underline** two reasons why the Constitution is important to United States citizens.

Tell what is happening in each picture.

Our Basic Rights

All citizens in the United States have **rights**, or things we are free to do. The government cannot take away these rights.

Citizens have the right to be treated as equals. This means we should each be treated the same way. The rules and laws in our country are the same for everyone.

Citizens have the right to vote. To **vote** means to make a choice about something. In the United States, citizens choose their leaders by voting. The people who get the most votes become our leaders.

Citizens vote to choose their leaders.

2. **Write** one right of citizens in our country.

_____

_____

_____

_____

The Bill of Rights

The Constitution does more than tell us how to run our government. It also tells us the rights shared by all United States citizens. Ten of these rights are listed in a part of the Constitution called the Bill of Rights. The Bill of Rights protects our freedom. **Freedom** is the right to choose what we do and say.

The Bill of Rights says that citizens in the United States are free to say and write what we want as long as it does not harm others. It also says that we can choose our own religion. We are free to meet other people in public places. We are free to speak up when we disagree with our government. We can ask our government to fix things we think are wrong.

3. Circle the rights you see in this picture.

Freedom is important to United States citizens. Many people think this is what makes our country a great place to live.

4. **Draw** something citizens can do because of their freedom.

5. ◉ **Main Idea and Details** What is the Bill of Rights?

_____

_____

_____

_____

6. ❓ Which right is the most important to you? **List** one reason for your choice.

_____

_____

_____

_____

⬛ **Stop!** I need help with _____

▶ **Go!** Now I know _____

We Follow Rules and Laws

Envision It!

Look at the pictures.

Think about a classroom where everyone is talking at the same time. Children are running around. No one takes turns or shares. This would not be a good place to learn.

School Rules

Your school has rules that help make it a good place for you to learn. Rules remind us how to be good school citizens. Rules also keep us safe. One rule tells us to take turns when talking. Another rule tells us not to run in the hall. You show respect for others and yourself when you follow rules.

1. **Write** one rule you follow at school.

_____

_____

_____

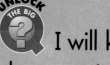

Write what these pictures tell you about some rules in a community.

Community Laws

Rules in a community are called laws. A **law** is a rule that everyone must follow. Leaders in our communities help make the laws.

Laws help keep us safe. It is the law that cars and bikes have to stop at a stop sign. Wearing a seat belt is an important law in many places in the United States. There is also a law that says people should not make a lot of noise at night.

Laws remind people to be responsible. In many places, the law says people may not throw trash on the street. This law helps keep the community clean.

2. ◎ **Main Idea and Details**
   <u>Underline</u> two community laws.

Most states have laws that say we must wear seat belts.

Why Laws Are Important

Laws are important because they protect our rights and keep us safe from harm. When the laws are not followed, people can get hurt.

In many places, it is a law to wear a helmet when you ride a bike. Following that law helps keep you safe. Drivers of cars must follow laws, too. They must stop at crosswalks and stop signs.

When people do not follow laws they might have to go to a court. A **court** is one part of our government. People who work in courts decide if someone has broken, or not followed, the law.

3. Draw an X on laws you see in this picture.

A **consequence** is something that happens as a result of an action. A person who breaks the law can have rights taken away. They might be required to pay a fine, or money, to the community. These consequences remind us that good citizens are responsible for their actions and respect the rights of others.

NO LITTERING VIOLATORS WILL BE PROSECUTED

4.  **Cause and Effect** <u>Underline</u> one thing that can happen when people do not follow laws.

Got it?

5.  **Draw Conclusions** Why is it important to have laws?

_____

_____

_____

6.  **Write** two laws in your community.   **my Story Ideas**

_____

_____

_____

 Stop! I need help with _____

▶ **Go!** Now I know _____

Draw Conclusions

Details give us information about something.

To draw a conclusion, we think about details or facts and come to a decision about what the details and facts mean.

Detail: The children make snow angels.

Detail: The children help shovel snow off the sidewalk.

Conclusion: The children like to be outside in the snow.

Detail: The children build a snowman.

Look at the pictures below and read the details.
Write a conclusion about laws on the lines below.

Detail: It is a law to wear a seat belt in a car.

Detail: People must wear helmets when they ride bikes.

Detail: It is a law that drivers must stop at stop signs.

Conclusion:

_____
_____
_____
_____
_____

Our Government

Look at the picture.

These workers are fixing a road. This service keeps drivers safe.

A government is a group of people who work together to run a community, state, or country. The Constitution tells us that citizens of the United States are responsible for their government. Citizens vote for leaders who will make good decisions that keep us safe and protect our rights.

Community Government

A community government works for people in a city or town. They solve problems and make sure that citizens have the services they need. A **service** is something helpful that is done for you. Schools, libraries, and fire stations are community services. Citizens pay **taxes,** or money, to the government to pay for these services.

1. **Underline** two things a community government does.

Put a ☑ on the places you have in your community.

UNLOCK THE BIG ?

I will know how the government gives communities what they need.

Vocabulary

service   Congress
tax   Supreme Court

State Government

A state government makes decisions that affect all the communities in one state. Different communities have different needs. A small town might need only one school, but a big city would need many.

The government of each state is located in its capital city. Leaders of state government make laws and decide which services to provide for its citizens. A police department is one service all states have. The police protect the people in the state.

2. ◎ **Main Idea and Details** **Underline** two services that are provided by state governments.

This is the state capitol building in Pennsylvania.

Congress meets
to vote on laws.

United States Government

Our government has three parts, called branches. Each branch has a different job. The president is the head of the first branch of our country's government. The president leads the country and signs new laws.

The second branch of government is Congress. **Congress** is made up of leaders who write and vote on new laws. Citizens in each state vote for their members of Congress. Members of Congress work in the Capitol, a building in Washington, D.C.

Courts are the third branch of government. The **Supreme Court** is the highest court in our country. Nine Supreme Court judges decide if the laws are fair. They also make sure that laws agree with the Constitution.

Supreme Court judges

3. Write the job for each branch of government.

Branches of Government	
President	
Congress	
Supreme Court	

4. ◎ **Draw Conclusions** Why do citizens pay taxes?

_____

_____

5. ❓ Why should citizens tell leaders what services they need?

_____

_____

_____

■ **Stop!** I need help with _____

▶ **Go!** Now I know _____

Our Leaders

Envision It!

Circle the community leader in each picture.

Government leaders work to make our cities, states, and country better places for citizens to live. They also help make laws. Good leaders should be honest and fair.

Community Leaders

The **mayor** is a government leader in a town or city. Many mayors make decisions and solve problems. Some places have a council. **Council** members are community citizens who work with the mayor. Citizens vote to choose their mayor and council.

The mayor and the council make laws for a community. They work together to make sure that each neighborhood in a community has services it needs, such as schools, fire departments, and clean water.

TOWN COUNCIL

1. **Underline** the group of citizens who work with the mayor for the community.

Draw a leader in your community.

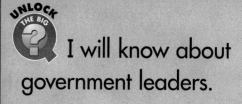
Vocabulary

mayor
council
governor

State Leaders

The **governor** is the leader of a state.
The governor works with other state leaders.
The citizens in each state vote to elect,
or choose, their state leaders.

The governor and other state leaders
make laws that everyone in the state must
follow. They decide how to spend money
for the state. They might decide to open
a state park or build a new highway.

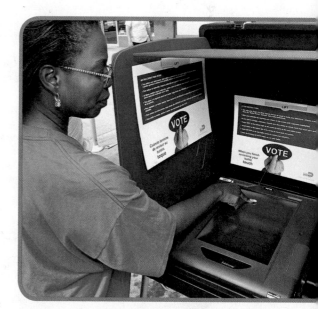

Citizens vote for
the governor.

2. ◉ **Fact and Opinion Read** the
sentences. **Put** an "F" if the sentence
is a fact. **Put** an "O" if it is an opinion.

The governor is the leader of a state. _____

The governor likes to live in the city. _____

The United States President

The president is the leader of our country. Citizens vote once every four years to choose our president.

The president works in our country's capital. Our country's capital is Washington, D.C. Every state has a capital, too.

3. **Look** at the map. **Mark** an X on our country's capital. (Circle) the capital of your state.

United States Capitals

Washington
★Olympia

★Salem
Oregon

Montana
★Helena

North Dakota
★Bismarck

Minnesota

New Hampshire

Vermont

Maine
★Augusta

Montpelier★ Concord
Albany★ ★Massachusetts
New York★ ★Boston
Hartford★ ★Providence
Rhode Island
Connecticut

★Boise
Idaho

Wyoming

South Dakota
Pierre★

St. Paul★ Wisconsin
Madison★

Michigan
Lansing★

Pennsylvania
Harrisburg ★
Columbus Annapolis
Ohio★ Trenton★ New Jersey
Dover
Delaware

Carson
★City
★Sacramento
Nevada

Salt Lake★
City
Utah

Cheyenne
★

Denver ★
Colorado

Nebraska
Lincoln★

Iowa
Des Moines★

Indiana
Indianapolis★

Springfield ★
Illinois

West
Virginia
Charleston★

Maryland
Washington, D.C.
Virginia

California

Arizona

Santa Fe
★

Topeka★
Kansas

★Jefferson
City
Missouri

★Frankfort Richmond★

Kentucky

Raleigh★ North
Carolina

★Phoenix

New
Mexico

Oklahoma
Oklahoma★
City

Arkansas
Little★
Rock

Tennessee
★Nashville

Columbia
South
Carolina

Texas

Louisiana
Baton
Rouge★

Mississippi
★Jackson

Alabama ★
Montgomery★
Atlanta

Georgia

★Austin

★Tallahassee

Florida

Alaska

Juneau★

★Honolulu
Hawaii

N
W E
S

Key

National Capital

★ State Capital

36

It is the president's job to make sure that citizens follow laws. The president also signs new laws created by Congress. The president nominates judges for the Supreme Court. The president works with leaders from other countries, too.

President Barack Obama in the Oval Office

4. **Underline** two things the president does as leader of our country.

5. **Draw Conclusions** Why do you think citizens might vote for the same leader many different times?

_____

_____

_____

_____

6. How do leaders help communities?

my Story Ideas

_____

_____

_____

_____

Stop! I need help with _____

Go! Now I know _____

Our Country's Symbols

Envision It!

The United States flag is important to citizens.

The United States has many symbols. A **symbol** is an object that stands for something else.

Our Country's Flag

Look at the picture of our country's flag above. The United States flag is a symbol of freedom. There are 50 stars and 13 stripes on our country's flag. Each star stands for one of our 50 states. The stripes stand for the first 13 states.

At school we say the Pledge of Allegiance to show we are proud to be American citizens. Americans believe that good citizens and leaders are fair, honest, and loyal.

1. **Underline** three words that describe good citizens.

The Pledge of Allegiance

I pledge allegiance to the flag of the United States of America and to the Republic for which it stands, one nation, under God, indivisible, with liberty and justice for all.

UNLOCK THE BIG ?

I will know our country's symbols.

Vocabulary

symbol
anthem
motto
independence

Write two things you see on the flag.

Our Country's Songs

Our country has a national **anthem,** or song. This song is called "The Star Spangled Banner." It is about our flag. The last part of the song says the United States is "...the land of the free and the home of the brave."

"America the Beautiful" is a song about the many beautiful places you can see in the United States. We sing these songs to show we are proud to be Americans.

2. ◉ **Draw Conclusions Write** what these songs tell visitors to our country about American citizens.

The United States flag

The Great
Seal of the
United States and
a penny both show
symbols of our country.

More Symbols of Our Country

Our country has many other symbols. The bald eagle, which lives only in North America, is another symbol of our country. There is a picture of the bald eagle on The Great Seal of the United States. This seal also shows our country's motto. A **motto** is a saying that stands for an important idea. Our country's motto is *E pluribus unum,* or "Out of many, one." These words tell citizens that we are one country made up of different states and different people. You can see our motto on coins, too.

3. **Circle** the motto on the picture of the Great Seal of the United States.

Mount Rushmore

Symbols of our country can be found in places, too. Mount Rushmore is in South Dakota. It is a mountain with the faces of four famous presidents carved on it.

The Liberty Bell

Long ago, the people who lived in America chose to fight for independence. **Independence** is freedom from being ruled by someone else. The Liberty Bell was made to celebrate this decision. You can visit the Liberty Bell in Philadelphia, Pennsylvania.

4. **Underline** two places where symbols can be found.

Got it?

5. ◉ **Main Idea and Details List** two symbols of our country.

_____

_____

_____

6. ❓ What do our country's symbols tell us   my Story Ideas
   about being good citizens and good leaders?

_____

_____

_____

⬛ **Stop!** I need help with _____

▶ **Go!** Now I know _____

Lesson 1

1. **Write** one way you can be a good citizen at school.

_____

- -

_____

- -

_____

Lesson 2

2. **Draw** a picture showing a right citizens have. **Fill in** the blank at the bottom of the picture.

Citizens have the right to _____

_____

3. Look at the picture. **Draw** a person following a law.

The laws says we have to wear a seat belt when we are in a car.

4. ◎ **Draw Conclusions** Why is it important to follow laws?

5. (Circle) the picture that shows a government service.

Lesson 5

6. Fill in the bubble next to the correct answer.

A governor is the leader of a

Ⓐ town   Ⓒ state

Ⓑ city   Ⓓ country

Lesson 6

7. List three words that describe a good citizen.

8. Draw a symbol of the United States. **Label** your drawing.

Go online to write and illustrate your own **myStory Book** using the **myStory Ideas** from this chapter.

 **How do people best cooperate?**

In this chapter you have learned what it means to be a good citizen and to help others. You learned the role of the government and how government helps communities.

© **w.2.6** Use digital tools for writing.

Think about your community. Is there a problem in your community? How could you fix it?

Draw a picture showing how you can cooperate with others to solve the problem. **Write** a caption.

While you're online, check out the **myStory Current Events** area where you can create your own book on a topic that's in the news.

Working to Meet Our Needs

How do people get what they need?

Draw a picture of you and your family or friends having a meal together.

my Story Video

 # Begin With a Song

What We Buy

Sing to the tune of "Twinkle, Twinkle, Little Star."

All producers try and try,
To make things we want to buy.

Then they ship them to the store,
For consumers to explore.

A decision must be made,
Then the final bill gets paid.

Vocabulary Preview

needs

wants

resource

cost

goods

producer

Circle examples of these words in the picture.

consumer

skill

trade

savings

borrow

loan

Needs and Wants

☐   ☐

Mark examples of things you must have to live with a check mark.

All people have needs and wants. **Needs** are things we must have to live. Food, clothing, and shelter are needs. **Wants** are things that we would like to have, but do not need to live. How do we get the things we need and want?

Getting What We Need and Want

We use resources to get things we need and want. A **resource** is something that we can use. Some resources come from nature, like water and plants. Money is also a resource. Most people work to earn money to buy the things they need and want.

1. **Look** at the photograph. **Write** the letter *N* on a need, and the letter *W* on a want.

Vocabulary

needs   scarce

wants

resource

Mark examples of things it would be nice to have with an X.

Making Choices

We cannot have everything we want. This is because resources are limited. For example, there is usually a limit to how much money we have. So, we often have to make choices.

Carlos likes music. He wants to learn to play the harmonica. He also wants an MP3 player. Carlos will have to choose between buying the harmonica and the MP3 player. He does not have enough money to buy both.

MP3 player

2. **Look** at the photographs. **Circle** what you would choose. **Tell** a partner why.

Harmonica

Families Make Choices

Families have to make choices about their needs and wants, too. Sometimes, resources are scarce. **Scarce** means there is not enough of something.

Families take care of the things they need first. What kind of food is best for us? Which clothes will keep us warm and dry? Where will we live?

Then families make choices about what they want. Games, treats, trips, and toys are some things families might want.

3. ◉ **Draw Conclusions** **Write** a sentence about the picture using *want* or *need*.

Communities Make Choices

People in a community make choices about how to use resources. People in this picture will decide how to use this school land. They will choose to plant a garden or build a playground. There is not enough land to do both.

4. (Circle) the area in the picture that shows the resource that is scarce.

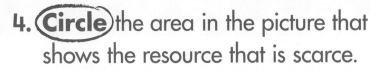

5. ◉ **Main Idea and Details** What does it mean when we say that resources can be scarce?

_____

_____

_____

_____

6. ❓ **List** two wants that you would like to buy. **my Story Ideas**

_____

_____

_____

■ **Stop!** I need help with _____

▶ **Go!** Now I know _____

Making Good Choices

Envision It!

Circle the two items you would buy.

People and communities make choices every day about how to use resources. How do they decide which choice is best? Let's see how some choices are made.

What Is the Choice?

The Archer family has money to spend on a family activity. First, they talk about things they like to do. Then, they come up with two choices.

The Archers will visit the science center or buy a new board game. They only have enough money to pay for one of these things. How will they decide which to choose?

1. ◎ **Cause and Effect** <u>Underline</u> the reason the Archers will make a choice.

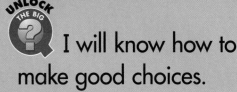

Vocabulary

benefit

cost

opportunity cost

Tell a partner why you chose the items.

Steps for Making Choices

First, the Archers will talk about the benefits of each choice. A **benefit** is a good result from a choice you make. At the science center, the Archers can learn about how things work and do fun experiments. The game can last for a long time. It can be shared with friends, too.

Next, the family will talk about the costs of each choice. The **cost** is the price of something. The science center tickets cost $48. The game costs $35.

Then, after thinking about the benefits and costs, they will make their choice. What would you choose?

2. Write 1, 2, or 3 next to each paragraph above to show the order of the steps.

Benefits and Costs

The Archers made a chart to help them choose.
A chart can help you make a decision. It shows
information clearly. The Archers listed the costs
and benefits of each choice.

3. Read the benefits. **Mark** an X in the box
for the activity you would choose.

What Should We Choose?			
Activity	Benefits	Cost	Choice
Family Game	1. Can use the game for a long time 2. Can share the game with friends	$35	☐
Science Center	1. Will learn how things work 2. Can do experiments	$48	☐

Opportunity Cost

If you can choose only one thing, you give up something else. The thing you give up when you make a choice is called the **opportunity cost.** The Archer family chose to go to the science center. They lost the opportunity to buy the game.

4. **Underline** the opportunity cost of the Archers' choice.

5. ◉ **Main Idea and Details** What is one thing you can think about before you make a choice?

_____

_____

_____

_____

6. You have enough money to go to the movies or to buy a book. **Circle** your choice. **Underline** the opportunity cost.

my Story Ideas

_____

⬛ **Stop!** I need help with _____

▶ **Go!** Now I know _____

Producing and Consuming Goods

Look at the pictures of the baker making pretzels.

Goods are things that people make or grow. Your family uses and buys goods. Goods are everything from tomatoes to televisions to trucks!

A person who makes or grows goods is a **producer.** A person who buys and uses goods is a **consumer.**

1. **Look** at the photograph. **Write** a *P* on the producer and a *C* on the consumer.

Producing Goods

People produce goods to earn money. Money that people earn is called **income.** Income is used to buy things people need and want.

This farmer sells tomatoes. The money she gets is her income.

Draw what happens next.

Vocabulary

goods   consumer
producer   income

Deciding What to Produce

Producers grow or make goods that consumers want to buy. Read about Farmer Green.

Farmer Green grows berries. She must decide if she should grow strawberries or blueberries. She learns that there are already a lot of blueberry farms in her community. Consumers can buy blueberries easily. There are not many strawberry farms.

People in her community will probably buy strawberries from Farmer Green if they cannot buy them from other producers. She will be able to sell a lot of strawberries at a good price.

2. ◎ **Main Idea and Details** Underline a detail that tells why Farmer Green might decide to grow strawberries.

Natural Resources

A natural resource is something useful that comes from the earth. Air, water, sunlight, and soil are all natural resources. Farmer Green needs soil and water to grow her strawberries.

3. **Underline** the definition of natural resource.

Other Kinds of Resources

Farmer Green needs other kinds of resources, too. She needs money and farm equipment. They are called capital resources. The tractor shown is a capital resource. She needs people to help plant and pick the strawberries. Workers are called human resources. Farmer Green needs natural, capital, and human resources to grow and sell strawberries.

Workers pick the strawberries when they are ripe. Then they put them on a truck that carries them to a market. Farmer Green, the producer, earns money selling the berries. The consumer buys the strawberries. Everyone gets something they want!

4. **Underline** two ways human resources are helpful on Farmer Green's farm.

Got it?

5. ◉ **Main Idea and Details** **List** three kinds of resources.

_____

_____

6. ❓ **Describe** a place you go to buy food.

_____

_____

_____

_____

⬜ **Stop!** I need help with _____

_____

▶ **Go!** Now I know _____

Reading a Flow Chart

A flow chart shows the order in which things happen. Each box shows a step. Each arrow points to the next step.

Look at the flow chart below. Read the title. It tells what the flow chart shows. This flow chart shows oranges as they are picked, squeezed, and then sold to consumers as juice.

Point to the first step. Tell what happens first. Follow the arrow with your finger. Tell what happens next. Follow the arrow with your finger. What is happening in the last step?

How We Get Orange Juice

Producers grow oranges in orchards. They pick them when they are ripe.

Oranges are squeezed at a factory. Juice goes into cartons.

Trucks bring cartons of juice to stores. Consumers buy the juice.

Try it!

1. **Describe** why a flow chart is helpful.

   _____

   _____

   _____

   _____

   _____

2. **Draw** pictures to complete the flow chart below. Add steps that show a family eating and cleaning up after dinner. **Mark** an arrow between the boxes to show the order in which things happen.

Having Dinner Together

Service Workers and Their Jobs

Look at the photographs. These people help others in their community.

Services are jobs that people do to help others. Sometimes people are paid money for their services. They are called service workers.

Services in the Community

In every community, many people work to provide, or give, services. Police officers, school nurses, and librarians are all service workers. Service workers are often paid for the services they do.

Taxi drivers, truck drivers, and street sweepers all provide services on our roads. Can you think of other people who provide services in your community?

1. **Underline** a service worker you have seen in your community.

A road crew provides a service by fixing our roads.

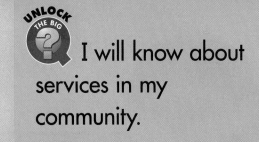
Vocabulary

skill

specialize

Draw a picture of someone who helps people in your community.

Special Skills

Doctors and nurses provide an important service. They help people stay healthy. They help people who are sick to get better.

Doctors and nurses need special skills to help people. A **skill** is knowing how to do something. Doctors need to know how to use special equipment to listen to people's hearts. They also use equipment to look inside people's ears, and to weigh people.

Many doctors specialize in one area. To **specialize** means to do one kind of thing very well. We visit some doctors for problems with our eyes, and other doctors when we break a bone.

2. **Underline** a special skill above.

Other Service Workers

We also have service workers in our schools. Principals, nurses, librarians, cafeteria workers, janitors, and teachers work in our schools. These service workers all have skills that help them do their jobs.

Some teachers specialize in one subject like math, science, and reading. Other teachers have to know how to teach music or physical education.

3. **Write** the name of a worker at your school who specializes in one area.

_____

- - - - - - - - - - - - - - - - - -

Government Workers

Police officers and firefighters are government workers. Communities pay these workers with money from taxes. A tax is money collected by a government to pay for services. Government leaders such as mayors, governors, and even our president are paid from taxes, too.

People who work for the post office are government workers, too. They work hard to make sure people all over the United States receive mail.

4.  **Main Idea and Details**
   <u>**Underline**</u> three government workers.

Got it?

5. ◉ **Draw Conclusions** What is one reason it is important for some workers to have special skills?

_____

_____

_____

_____

6. ❓ How do we pay for community services?    **Story Ideas**

_____

_____

_____

⬛ **Stop!** I need help with _____

_____

▶ **Go!** Now I know _____

Main Idea and Details

When you read a paragraph, look for the main idea and details. The main idea tells you what a paragraph is about. Details tell you more about the main idea.

Read the letter below. The main idea is circled. The details are underlined.

Dear Mr. Patel,

I really liked art class this year.
I liked making pots with clay. It was
fun finger painting. Making flowers
with tissue paper was my favorite.
Thank you for being a great teacher.

Sincerely,

Susan Lester

Learning Objective
....
I will know how to identify the main idea
and details in a paragraph.

 **RI.2.6** Identify author's purpose for writing.

Try it!

Read the letter below. **Circle** the main idea.
Underline three details.

Dear Susan,

You are a talented art student. Your
clay pot will make a nice gift. Your
finger painting was very colorful.
Your tissue paper flowers were
lovely. Thank you for your kind letter.
Keep making great art!

Sincerely,

Mr. Patel

Trading for Goods and Services

Circle the goods in the photograph that the children trade.

How do we get the goods and services we need and want? We trade for them. **Trade** means to buy, sell, or exchange goods or services with someone else. Any place we trade for goods or services is called a market.

Trading Goods

When you go to the store, you probably use money to pay for the things you want. Long ago, people did not use money to buy things. They bartered goods to get what they needed. To **barter** is to trade goods or services without using money. Today, some people barter, but most people use money to buy what they need.

1. ◉ **Main Idea and Details**
   <u>Underline</u> a detail about trading goods.

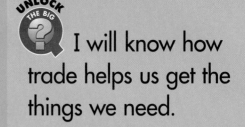

Draw something that you and a friend might trade with each other.

Vocabulary
....

trade   supply
barter
demand

Supply and Demand

Producers make choices about what to sell. They think about **demand,** or how many people want something. Then they think about **supply,** or how much of it there is. Together, supply and demand help producers decide how much they can charge for their product.

Pat loves to eat fish, but she lives in a city that is not near water. Not many places near Pat's home sell fish. A lot of people want fish, so the people who sell it can charge a high price.

Pat's grandmother lives by the ocean. When Pat visits her, she gets to eat a lot of fish. Producers who sell fish cannot charge a high price or people would buy from someone else.

2. **Underline** two reasons why fish costs more in Pat's city.

Trade in the United States

People in one state can trade goods with people in other states. Oranges grow in Florida. The winters there are warm. Soybeans grow in Iowa. The soil there is rich. So, producers in Florida can sell oranges to consumers in Iowa. Producers in Iowa can sell soybeans to consumers in Florida.

3. **Look** at the map. **Write** one way for consumers in Illinois to get oranges.

United States Trade

Key

- major orange-producing state
- major soybean-producing state

Trade With Other Countries

Some goods and services that people in the United States use are not produced here. We can trade goods and services with people in other countries to get the things we use. There are not many places in the United States where bananas grow well. The bananas you eat might have come from Ecuador.

4. **Underline** a country that trades with the United States.

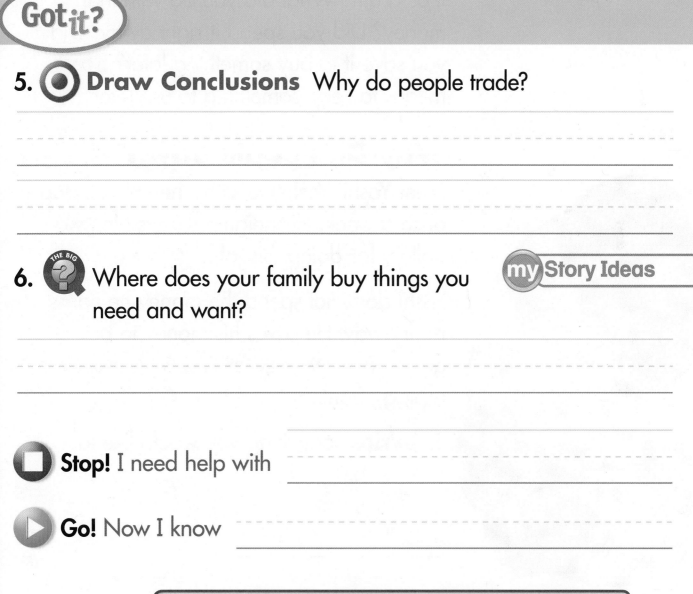

Got it?

5. ◉ **Draw Conclusions** Why do people trade?

_____

_____

_____

_____

6. ❓ Where does your family buy things you need and want?   my Story Ideas

_____

- -

_____

⬛ **Stop!** I need help with - - - - - - - - - - - - - - - -

▶ **Go!** Now I know - - - - - - - - - - - - - - - - -

Making Choices About Money

Envision It!

START TO SAVE TODAY!

My Savings

Write an *S* on the picture that shows someone saving money.

Have you ever earned money or received it as a gift? What did you do with that money? Did you spend it right away? Did you save it to buy something later? **Save** means to keep something to use later.

Why Do People Save?

Meet Yoshi. Yoshi walks his neighbor's dog once a week. His neighbor pays him two dollars for doing this job.

Yoshi does not spend the money he earns right away. He saves his money to buy a game. Every week, Yoshi puts his money in a piggy bank.

1. **Write** something you would like to save for.

_____

_____

Vocabulary

save

savings

borrow

loan

Write an *SP* on the picture that shows someone spending money.

A Savings Plan

The money in Yoshi's piggy bank is called savings. **Savings** is money that you do not spend right away. When Yoshi has enough savings, he will buy the game.

Yoshi has a savings plan. A savings plan helps people set goals for how much money to save. If Yoshi saves the money he earns each week, instead of spending it, he will be able to buy the game.

The game Yoshi wants costs $8. Look at Yoshi's savings plan. Yoshi's savings plan shows that if he saves all of his money from walking dogs, he will be able to buy the game in four weeks.

2. **Write** the total amount Yoshi will save in four weeks on the savings plan.

Yoshi's Savings Plan

Week	Saved
Week 1	$2
Week 2	$2
Week 3	$2
Week 4	$2
Total =	

Kate's grandfather helps her open a savings account.

Saving at a Bank

Yoshi's friend Kate is also saving money. Kate earns money by raking her neighbor's yard. She wants to save her money. Her grandfather took her to a bank to open a savings account. A savings account is money saved in a bank. It will not get lost or stolen. Kate's money is safe in the bank.

3. ⦿ **Draw Conclusions**
   <u>Underline</u> one reason that people save money at a savings bank.

Borrowing Money

Sometimes people need to buy something right away, but do not have enough money. They may decide to borrow money from a bank. **Borrow** means to use something now and give it back later. When people borrow money, that money is called a **loan.** They will need to pay back the loan at a later time.

Sometimes Kate's grandfather uses a credit card to buy things.

People can also get credit cards from a bank to buy things. Using a credit card is the same as getting a loan.

Sometimes Kate's grandfather uses a credit card to buy things. Kate's grandfather will pay the credit card bill at the end of the month. The bank will get back the money it loaned.

4. Fill in the blank. Money you borrow is called a _____

Got it?

5. ◉ **Main Idea and Details** What is one reason people save their money?

_____

_____

_____

_____

6. ❓ What could you buy if you saved for a long time? How would you save the money?

my Story Ideas

_____

_____

_____

_____

■ **Stop!** I need help with _____

▶ **Go!** Now I know _____

Review and Assessment

Lesson 1

1. **Fill in** the bubble next to the correct answer. Which item below is a want?

   Ⓐ shoes

   Ⓑ cell phone

   Ⓒ apple

   Ⓓ water

2. **Write** why the item is not a need.

   _____

   _____

   _____

Lesson 2

3. A box of markers costs $8. A new t-shirt costs $17. **Write** the item you would choose and a benefit for your choice.

   _____

   _____

   _____

4. ◉ **Main Idea and Details** Why do producers need to sell things that consumers will buy?

5. Look at the pictures. **Write** *goods* or *services* under each picture to tell whether the person provides a good or a service.

6. (Circle) the picture that shows bartering. **Underline** the picture that shows people using money to trade.

7. Why do people trade with people from other states and countries?

_____

_____

_____

Lesson 6

8. Why do people save money?

_____

_____

_____

_____

Go online to write and illustrate your own **myStory Book** using the **myStory Ideas** from this chapter.

How do people get what they need?

In this chapter you have learned about how people provide goods and services. You also learned how people are able to get those goods and services.

© **W.2.6** Use digital tools for writing.

What is a good or service you would like to provide to earn income when you grow up?

Draw a picture that shows you selling a good or providing a service. Include the people who are buying your goods or using your service. **Write** a caption for your picture.

While you're online, check out the **myStory Current Events** area where you can create your own book on a topic that's in the news.

The World Around Us

 What is the world like?

Draw a picture of the place where you live.

my Story Video

 Begin With a Song

Places Where We Live

by Charlotte Munez

Sing to the tune of "On Top of Old Smokey."

We live in big cities
And suburbs or towns.
These places are different
In their sights and their sounds.

Big cities and small towns
Are found everywhere.
A road or a highway
Will take you right there!

Vocabulary Preview

symbol

continent

ocean

landform

weather

environment

(Circle) examples
of these words in
the picture.

rural

natural resource

renewable

conserve

technology

transportation

Talking About Location

Mark the picture of the bird under a branch with an **X**.

Look around. What do you see? Everything around you is in a certain location, or place. Location tells where something is.

Relative Location

Are you sitting near or far from the door to your classroom? **Relative location** tells where something is by comparing it to something else. Location words like *above, below, next to, near,* and *far* tell the relative location of people, places, and things. The picture shows buildings in a town.

1. **Circle** the building next to the bakery.

Mark the picture of the bird above a branch with a ✓.

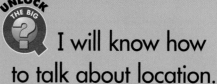
Vocabulary

relative location
absolute location
grid map

Absolute Location

How does a postal worker know where to deliver a letter? The address on a letter tells the absolute location of a place, such as a home or school. An **absolute location** is the exact spot where a place is located. A postal worker uses absolute location to make sure that every letter is delivered to the right place.

2. ◎ **Main Idea and Details Look** at the Rainbow Restaurant in the picture. **Write** the absolute location of the Rainbow Restaurant.

_____

_____

Maps Show Locations

This photograph shows Washington, D.C. A map can show what a place looks like from above.

The map below shows Washington, D.C. This map has a grid. A **grid map** has lines that cross to make squares. Columns are labeled across the bottom with letters. Rows are labeled along the side with numbers. The square where a column and a row meet tells the location of a place. Squares are named by their column and row. So, the square in the top right corner is called D1.

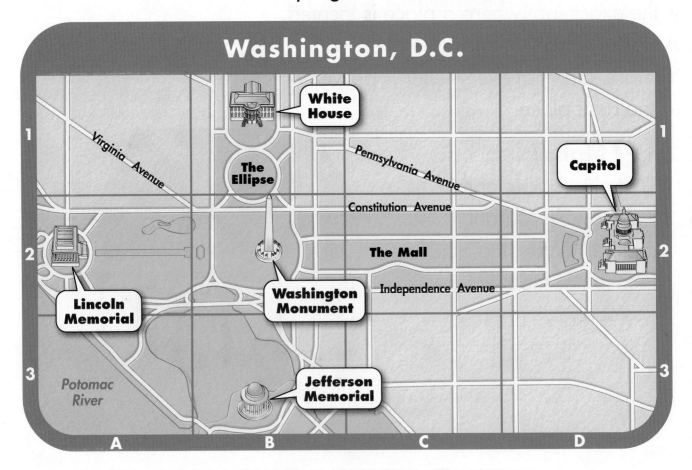

Washington, D.C.

White House

Capitol

Virginia Avenue

The Ellipse

Pennsylvania Avenue

Constitution Avenue

The Mall

Independence Avenue

Lincoln Memorial

Washington Monument

Jefferson Memorial

Potomac River

3. Write the letter and number for the square on the map where the White House is located. _____

4. Write the name of the building in square D2.

_____

_____

Got it?

5. ◎ **Compare and Contrast** Compare and contrast absolute location and relative location.

_____

_____

_____

_____

_____

6. ❓ **Write** a relative location for your desk.   my Story Ideas

_____

_____

_____

⬛ **Stop!** I need help with _____

▶ **Go!** Now I know _____

All About Maps

Envision It!

Look at the mountain.
Draw a simple shape to show the mountain.

Maps can show many different things. A map can show natural things, such as land and water. A map can also show things that people have put on the land, such as roads and buildings.

Why We Use Maps

Maps show information about an area. There are many different kinds of maps. The family in the photograph is using a map to follow a trail. The map also shows which direction to go to find the closest picnic area.

1. **Draw** a simple map of your classroom.

Look at the bridge.
Draw a simple shape to show the bridge.

I will know how to use maps to locate places and things.

Vocabulary

symbol
cardinal direction
intermediate direction

Using the Parts of a Map

Point to the map title on the map below. It tells what place the map shows. Now look at the map. This map uses pictures to stand for real things. These pictures are called **symbols.** The key tells what each symbol on the map means.

2. **Draw** a line from each key symbol to its location on the map.

Rock Trail

Key

walking path

river

entrance

picnic area

ranger station

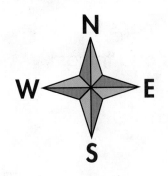

Cardinal Directions

A compass rose shows two kinds of directions. **Cardinal directions** are the four main directions. These are north, south, east, and west. Look at the compass rose. The letters *N*, *S*, *E*, and *W* stand for north, south, east, and west.

3. ◎**Main Idea and Details Look** at the map and use the compass rose. **Write** an *N* on the place that is north of Town Hall. **Circle** the place that is west of Town Hall.

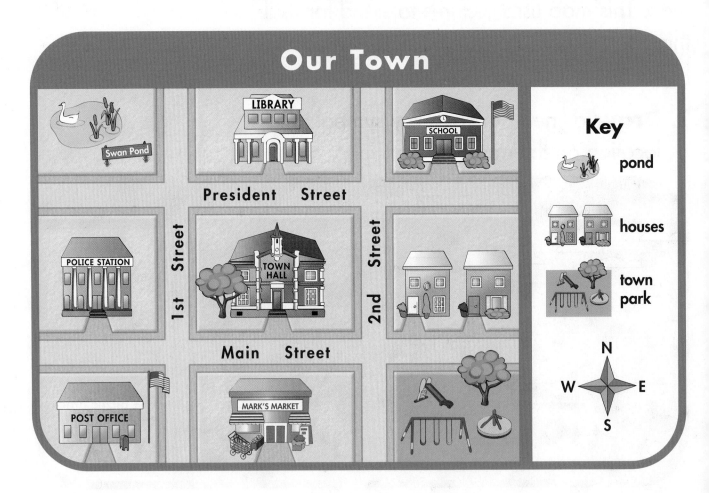

Intermediate Directions

The directions between the cardinal directions are the **intermediate directions.** These are northeast, southeast, southwest, and northwest. Each intermediate direction is shown with two letters. *NE, SE, SW,* and *NW* stand for northeast, southeast, southwest, and northwest.

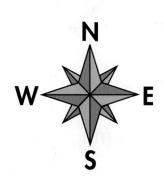

4. **Label** *NE, SE, SW,* and *NW* on the compass rose.

5. ◉ **Draw Conclusions** Why do people use maps?

_____

_____

_____

6. ❓ **List** something natural and something made by humans that you pass on your way to school.

_____

_____

_____

⬛ **Stop!** I need help with _____

▶ **Go!** Now I know _____

Using a Map Scale

A map is smaller than the real area on Earth it shows. You can use a map scale to figure out the distance, or amount of space, between two places. Look at the scale on this map of Florida. If you put a ruler under the scale, you will see that 1 inch stands for about 100 miles.

Florida, Political

Alabama

Georgia

Pensacola

Tallahassee ★

Jacksonville

Gainesville

ATLANTIC OCEAN

Ocala

Daytona Beach

Gulf of Mexico

Orlando

Tampa

| 0 | 50 | 100 | | 200 mi |
| 0 | | 200 km | | |

Sarasota

Lake Okeechobee

West Palm Beach

Ft. Myers

Ft. Lauderdale

Miami

Key

★ state capital

• city

N W E S

Key West

Follow the steps for using a map scale.

- Place a strip of paper from the dot by the city
  of Orlando to the dot by the city of Miami.
  Mark each dot on the strip of paper.

- Place the strip of paper along the map scale
  with one mark at zero.

- The other mark is at 200. That means the
  distance between Orlando and Miami is
  about 200 miles.

1. **Write** the distance in miles between
   Tallahassee and Tampa.

   _____

   -

   _____

2. **Draw** a simple map of an area in your
   community. Include buildings, roads, and
   walkways on your map. Also include a title,
   map scale, key, and compass rose.

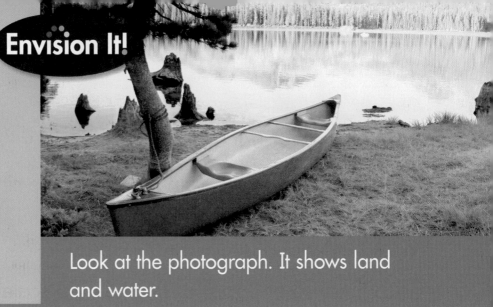

Envision It!

Look at the photograph. It shows land and water.

Earth has seven large areas of land called **continents.** They are North America, South America, Europe, Africa, Asia, Australia, and Antarctica. Earth has four bodies of water called **oceans** that cover most of its surface. They are the Atlantic Ocean, Pacific Ocean, Indian Ocean, and Arctic Ocean.

Earth From Far Away

This photograph shows Earth from outer space. You can see that Earth's shape is round, like a ball. Earth is very large. Because of Earth's shape, even a photograph taken from space can only show one part of Earth at a time.

1. ◎ **Cause and Effect** <u>Underline</u> the reason you cannot view all of Earth at one time.

Draw another picture that shows land and water.

I will know how Earth is shown on a globe and on a world map.

Vocabulary

continent
ocean
equator
prime meridian

Showing Earth on a Globe

One way to learn about something large is to look at a model, or small copy of the real thing. A globe is a model of Earth. If you spin a globe, you can see all of Earth's land and water.

Look at the North Pole and South Pole on the globe. It is very cold in both of these locations. Now, look for the equator. The **equator** is an imaginary line that divides Earth in half. The northern half is called the Northern Hemisphere. The southern half is called the Southern Hemisphere. People who live in the United States live in the Northern Hemisphere.

2. **Write** the letter *N* on the Northern Hemisphere, and the letter *S* on the Southern Hemisphere.

North Pole

equator

South Pole

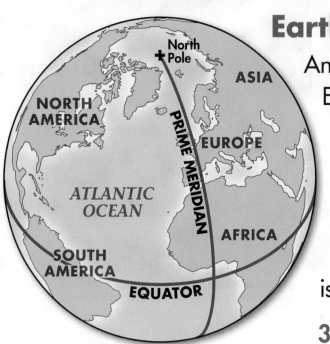

Earth East and West

Another imaginary line that divides Earth in half is called the **prime meridian.** Find the prime meridian on the globe. The half of Earth east of the prime meridian is the Eastern Hemisphere. The half of Earth west of the prime meridian is the Western Hemisphere.

3. **Write** the letter *E* on the Eastern Hemisphere.

Latitude and Longitude

A world map is a flat drawing of Earth. Mapmakers use a special grid system that helps us find the exact location of any place on Earth. This system uses two sets of imaginary lines that cross called lines of latitude and lines of longitude.

Lines that run east and west are lines of latitude. Lines that run north and south are lines of longitude. Places where lines of latitude and longitude cross are absolute locations.

4. **Write** what kind of line the equator is.

_____

_____

The World

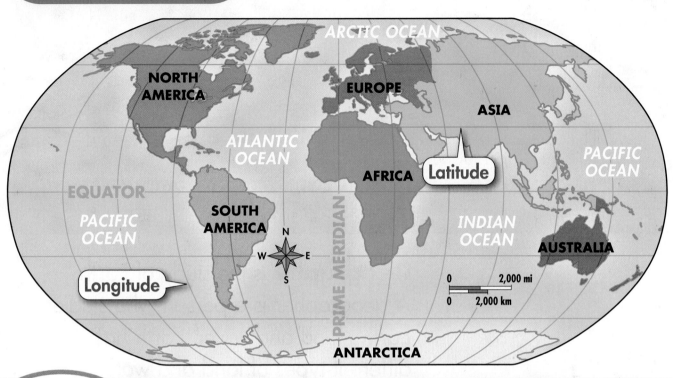

Got it?

5. ◉ **Main Idea and Details** **Write** one relative location of North America.

_____

_____

6. 🔍 Which ocean is closest to your home?   my Story Ideas ___

_____

⬜ **Stop!** I need help with _____

▶ **Go!** Now I know _____

Landforms and Bodies of Water

Envision It!

Look at the photographs. Draw a box around an activity done on land.

Geography is the study of Earth. A geographer is a person who studies Earth's land and water. Earth has different types of land and water.

Landforms

The shapes of Earth's land are called **landforms.** A mountain is the highest land on Earth. A hill is an area of raised land. It is like a mountain, but it is not as high. The low land between mountains or hills is called a valley.

A plain is a large area of flat land. Plains do not have big hills or mountains. A high plain is called a plateau. Plateaus are far above the level of the ocean.

1. ◎ **Draw Conclusions Write** *mountain* and *plain* on the landforms in the photograph.

100

UNLOCK THE BIG ?

I will know how to identify different kinds of land and water.

Vocabulary

geography
landform
physical map
political map

Circle an activity done on water.

Bodies of Water

Earth has two kinds of water, salt water and fresh water. Oceans have salt water. Rivers and lakes have fresh water. A river is a long body of water that flows into another body of water. A lake is a body of water surrounded by land.

2. **Underline** two kinds of water.

Land Meets Water

An island is a landform that has water on all sides. A peninsula has water on all sides but one. The place where land meets the ocean is called the coast.

3. **Write** a landform shown in the photograph.

_____

- - - - - - - - - - - - - - - - - - -

Physical Maps

Physical maps show Earth's land and water. The colors and symbols on a physical map show landforms, rivers, lakes, and oceans. The color blue is used to show water.

The physical map below shows landforms and bodies of water in the United States. The key on the map tells the color or symbol for landforms and bodies of water.

4. **Circle** the areas on the map that have mountains.

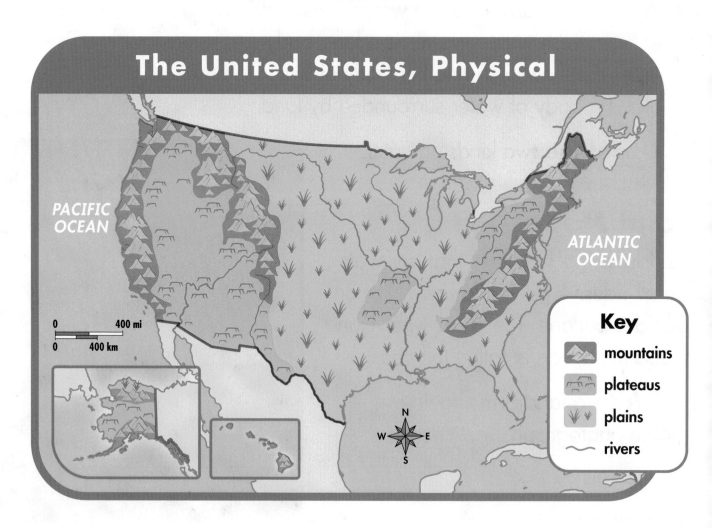

The United States, Physical

PACIFIC OCEAN

ATLANTIC OCEAN

0   400 mi
0   400 km

Key

mountains

plateaus

plains

rivers

Political Maps

Political maps show imaginary lines called borders. Towns, states, and countries all have borders. Look at the political map of North America. It shows the borders of the countries in North America.

5. **Circle** a border line on the map.

CANADA

PACIFIC OCEAN

UNITED STATES

ATLANTIC OCEAN

Gulf of Mexico

MEXICO

Caribbean Islands

Central America

N W E S

0   1,500 mi
0   1,500 km

Got it?

6. ⊙ **Main Idea and Details** **Circle** the countries and regions in North America on the map above.

7. **?** **Write** the name of one landform or body of water located in your community.

my **Story Ideas**

_____

_____

_____

■ **Stop!** I need help with _____

▶ **Go!** Now I know _____

Weather and Climate

Envision It!

Draw something you can use when it rains.

What is the weather today? **Weather** is what it is like outside at a certain time and place. Does the air feel cold or hot? We use the word **temperature** to talk about how hot or cold something is.

Wet and Dry Weather

Weather can also be wet or dry. Wet days are cloudy, with rain or snow. Snow falls when it is cold outside. On dry days, there is no rain or snow. Dry days are often sunny and clear. Clear means there are no clouds.

When the weather is cold and wet, we choose warm clothes. When the weather is hot and dry, we choose light clothes.

1. ◎ **Cause and Effect** (Circle) how you know the weather in the photograph is hot and dry.

Draw something you can use when it snows.

UNLOCK THE BIG ?

I will know how different kinds of weather affect people, animals, and plants.

Vocabulary

weather	climate
temperature	region

Weather and Nature

Animals and plants live and grow in different places. Polar bears are animals that live only where the weather is cold. Their heavy fur helps them stay warm in places that are cold and snowy.

Moss is a plant that grows in places where the weather is wet. A rainforest is a place with very wet weather. It can rain 14 feet in one year! Wet weather is good for frogs. It keeps their skin from getting too dry.

2. **Underline** how wet weather helps frogs.

Many frogs live in the Hoh Rainforest in Washington State.

Climate Regions

The weather a place has over a long time is called its **climate.** Climate affects the way people live. People who live in a cold, snowy climate often wear warm clothes and boots. For fun, they might ski and sled.

A **region** is an area that shares something alike. Some regions share the same climate. The map below shows five different climate regions in the United States.

3. **Outline** your state's climate region on the map. (Circle) your climate on the key.

United States Climate Regions

0   400 mi
0   400 km

Washington
Montana
North Dakota
Minnesota
New Hampshire
Vermont
Maine
Oregon
Idaho
South Dakota
Wisconsin
Michigan
New York
Massachusetts
Wyoming
Iowa
Pennsylvania
Rhode Island
Connecticut
Nevada
Nebraska
Indiana
Ohio
New Jersey
Utah
Illinois
West Virginia
Delaware
ATLANTIC OCEAN
California
Colorado
Kansas
Missouri
Maryland
Virginia
Washington, D.C.
Kentucky
North Carolina
Arizona
New Mexico
Oklahoma
Arkansas
Tennessee
South Carolina
PACIFIC OCEAN
Texas
Alabama
Mississippi
Georgia
Louisiana
Florida
Gulf of Mexico

N
W   E
S

Alaska
Hawaii

Key

marine
cold
warm and wet
hot and wet
hot and dry

106

Weather Changes

Weather changes every day. It may become cloudy, windy, or warm. Sudden weather changes can be dangerous. A lot of rain can cause a flood. Weather with strong winds is called a storm. Tornadoes and hurricanes are both dangerous kinds of storms.

4. **Underline** two dangerous storms.

Tornado

5. ◉ **Cause and Effect** How does weather affect you?

_____

_____

_____

_____

6. **THE BIG ?** What is the weather in your region today? **my Story Ideas**

_____

_____

_____

⏹ **Stop!** I need help with _____

▶ **Go!** Now I know _____

Our Environment

Envision It!

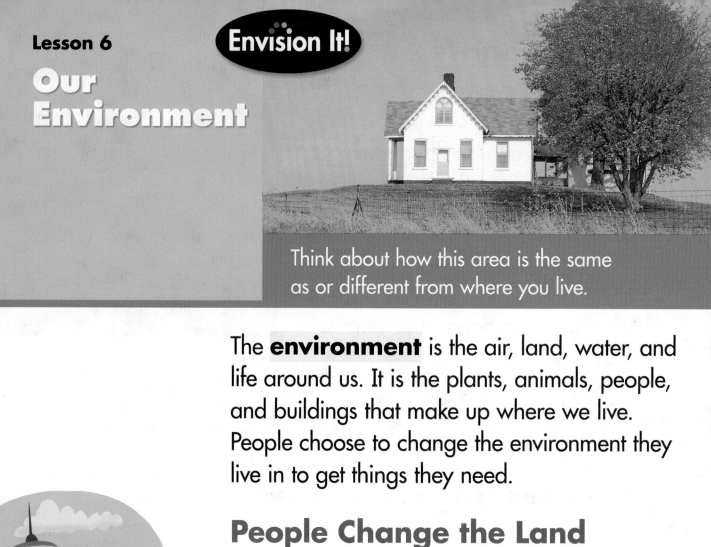

Think about how this area is the same as or different from where you live.

The **environment** is the air, land, water, and life around us. It is the plants, animals, people, and buildings that make up where we live. People choose to change the environment they live in to get things they need.

People Change the Land

People build cities on the land. A city is an **urban** environment. Most cities start small and then grow. In cities, people build highways, apartment buildings, and office buildings.

Draw a picture of where you live.

UNLOCK THE BIG ?

I will know ways that people change their environment.

Vocabulary
....
environment
urban
suburban
rural

Before building, people remove the trees and other plants. Animals must find other places to live. People use machines to make the land flat.

A **suburban** environment is close to a city. In the suburbs, people clear land to build roads, houses, parks, and shopping centers. A **rural** environment is made up of small towns and farms. Farmers clear land to plant crops.

1. ◎ **Compare and Contrast Write** *U, S,* and *R* where urban, suburban, and rural environments are shown.

Hoover Dam

People Change the Water

One way people change Earth's water is by building dams. A dam is a wall across a river or stream. Dams can hold water and create energy. People also change the water by building canals. A canal is a waterway that connects two bodies of water. Canals help people travel and move goods.

2. **Underline** two ways people change the water.

Making Life Easier

We change our environment to make life easier. These changes are important for how people work and live. Roads, bridges, and tunnels connect places so people can travel quickly from one place to another.

Pittsburgh, Pennsylvania

Farmers plow soil to plant seeds and grow crops. When there is not enough rain to grow crops, farmers irrigate their land. To irrigate means to move water to dry land. That makes it easier for everyone to have the food we need to live!

3. **Circle** the part of the picture that shows what *irrigate* means.

4. 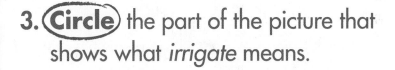 **Cause and Effect Write** an effect that changing the environment can have.

_____

_____

_____

5. 🄫 Is the environment where you live urban, suburban, or rural? **Write** one way you know.

my Story Ideas

_____

_____

_____

_____

⬛ **Stop!** I need help with _____

▶ **Go!** Now I know _____

Cause and Effect

A cause is the reason something happens.
The effect is what happens.

Look at the picture of rain. The rain is a cause.
Follow the arrow. It points to a picture showing
an umbrella. Rainy weather caused the boy to
open his umbrella. That is the effect.

© **RI.2.3** Describe connection among events.

Learning Objective
I will know how to recognize cause and effect.

Try it!

1. **Look** at the picture of people cleaning the beach. Are the people the cause or the effect?

   _____

   -

   _____

2. **Write** the effect.

   _____

   -

   _____

3. **Look** at the pictures below. **Draw** the missing effect and the missing cause in the empty boxes.

Cause   **Effect**

Cause   **Effect**

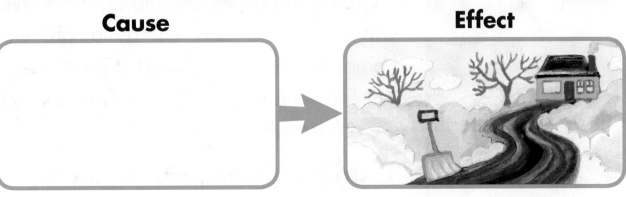

trees   wheat

Draw lines from the trees and the wheat to the product we make from them.

We get everything we need to live from nature. We get air to breathe and sunlight for energy. We even get oil to make gas for our cars. Nature is full of things for us to use. We call them **natural resources.**

Renewable Resources

A resource that can be replaced is called **renewable.** Water, wind, sunlight, and soil are all renewable resources. Natural processes can replace our water and soil. We will never run out of wind or sun.

Energy is the power used to do work. We can use wind to make energy to light our homes. When we use wind, it is not used up. The wind keeps blowing. That is why we call it renewable.

1. **Underline** the word that means "can be replaced."

Wind turbines make energy from wind.

UNLOCK THE BIG ?

I will know how to identify, use, and conserve resources.

Vocabulary

natural resource
renewable
nonrenewable
conserve

Nonrenewable Resources

A resource that cannot be replaced is called **nonrenewable.** Oil and coal are two nonrenewable resources. We can burn coal to make energy to light our homes. When we burn coal it is gone forever.

This pie chart shows how people in the United States use energy. A pie chart compares the amount of one thing to the amount of another. Use the pie chart to answer the question.

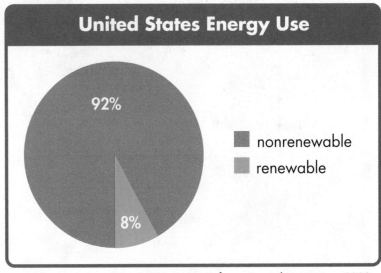

United States Energy Use

92%

8%

- nonrenewable
- renewable

Source: U.S. Energy Information Administration, 2009

2. **◎ Draw Conclusions Fill in** the blank.

In the United States, we get most of our energy

_____

from _____ resources.

States and Resources

Different states have different resources. The resources in a place affect how people live and work. This map shows some resources in the Southeast. Much of the land is used for farming. People there may grow crops or raise animals on farms. People who live near the coasts may have jobs fishing.

3. **Look** at the map. (Circle) the area of the Southeast where coal is mined.

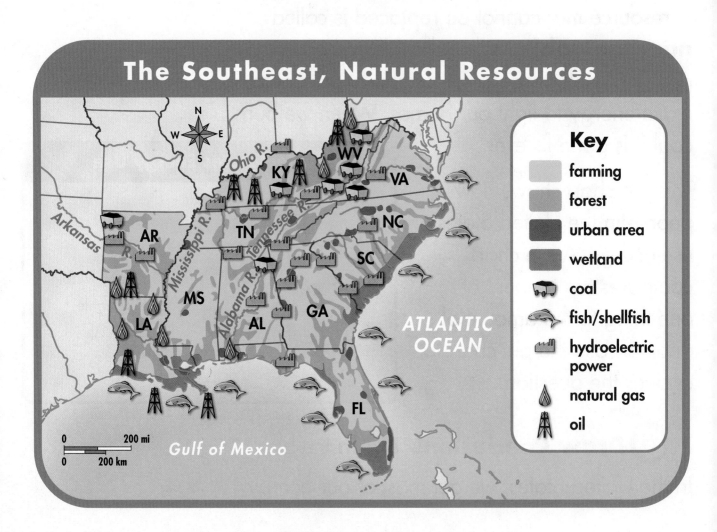

The Southeast, Natural Resources

Key

- farming
- forest
- urban area
- wetland
- coal
- fish/shellfish
- hydroelectric power
- natural gas
- oil

ATLANTIC OCEAN

Gulf of Mexico

0 — 200 mi
0 — 200 km

We Conserve Resources

Natural resources are important for our future. We need to **conserve,** or protect, the resources we use. Turn off the faucet to reduce the amount of water you use when you brush your teeth. Reuse plastic bags. Recycle paper, cans, plastic, and glass so they can be made into new things.

4. **Underline** two details that tell how you can conserve resources.

5. **Cause and Effect** Why do we conserve resources?

_____

_____

6. **Write** one natural resource that you use each day. How do you use it?

my **Story Ideas**

_____

_____

_____

_____

Stop! I need help with _____

Go! Now I know _____

Moving Ideas, People, and Things

These pictures show two ways that people can share their thoughts and ideas.

People, ideas, and goods move around the world every day. Technology makes these movements easier every year. **Technology** is the use of skills and tools.

Moving Ideas

Communication is the way people share ideas, thoughts, or information with each other. Today's technology makes communication fast and easy. You can use a computer to send letters, play games, learn, hear music, and watch movies. You can make a phone call from almost anywhere with a cell phone. A GPS, or global positioning system, is a way to tell someone your exact location anywhere in the world.

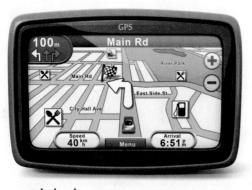

Global positioning system

1. **Cause and Effect** <u>Underline</u> one effect of new technology.

Draw a picture that shows a way to move people or goods.

Moving People

People move from place to place in many ways. **Transportation** is a way to move people and goods. We travel on buses, in taxis, on subways, or in cars. When we travel in cars, we use roads and highways. Road maps help us get from one place to another.

2. **Circle** Interstate 40 from Jackson to Nashville.

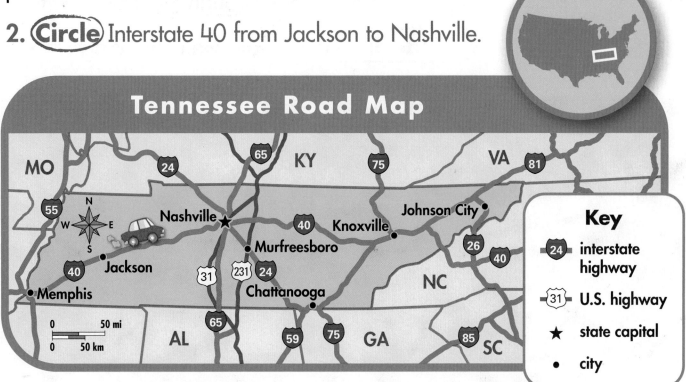

Tennessee Road Map

MO

24 65 KY 75 VA 81

55

N
W · E
S

Nashville ★

40 Knoxville Johnson City ·

Murfreesboro ·

40 Jackson

31 231 24

Chattanooga

NC

· Memphis

65 59 75 GA 85 SC

0 50 mi
0 50 km

AL

Key

24 interstate highway

31 U.S. highway

★ state capital

· city

Moving Things

Have you ever received a letter or a gift in the mail? How do you get groceries home from the store? Every day, people move big and small things from one place to another.

We make changes to the earth to make it easier to move things. We build roads. We blast tunnels through hills and mountains. We build bridges over rivers.

The United States cannot make or grow everything we need and want. Instead, we must trade with other countries. When we trade, we use transportation to move things. Trucks move goods over roads. Trains move goods across railways. Ships move goods across oceans. Airplanes move goods through the air.

3. **Underline** three ways we move things.

Helping One Another

We use communication and transportation to help people all over the world. When people need food or medicine, we can send help quickly. Helicopters send supplies to places that are hard to reach.

4. <u>Underline</u> two goods we can give to help people in need.

5. ◉ **Cause and Effect Write** a form of technology that has made communication or transportation easier.

_____

_____

_____

6. **THE BIG ?** How have you used transportation or communication today?

 my Story Ideas

_____

_____

_____

_____

■ **Stop!** I need help with _____

▶ **Go!** Now I know _____

Lesson 1

1. (Circle) the absolute location.

The front of the class   On the desk   14 Main Street

Lesson 2

2. Draw a compass rose.

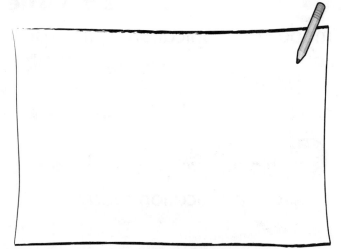

Lesson 3

3. Draw a line from each word to its location on the map.

equator

prime meridian

latitude

longitude

Lesson 4

4. Draw and label two kinds of landforms.

Lesson 5

5. ◉ **Cause and Effect Fill in** the bubble next to the correct answer.

Amelia wears a warm coat and hat when the weather is

ⓐ warm and sunny.

ⓒ hot and wet.

ⓑ cold and windy.

ⓓ hot and dry.

Lesson 6

6. Write two ways that people change their environment.

7. List four items you can recycle.

8. Write how two types of transportation help us.

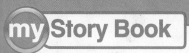
Go online to write and illustrate your own **myStory Book** using the **myStory Ideas** from this chapter.

 **What is the world like?**

In this chapter you have learned about Earth and the plants, animals, and people who live here.

What kinds of things can you do to help Earth stay healthy? **Draw** a picture showing what you can do. Add a caption.

© **W.2.6** Use digital tools for writing.

While you're online, check out the **myStory Current Events** area where you can create your own book on a topic that's in the news.

 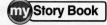

Celebrating Our Traditions

How is culture shared?

Think about stories your family tells. **Draw** a picture of how you celebrate your culture.

my Story Video

 # Begin With a Song

Festival Time

Sing to the tune of "Do Your Ears Hang Low?"

There's a festival,
Please come along with me.
We'll attend a ceremony,
There's a lot to do and see.
We can learn about our culture.
What a fun time it will be,
At the festival.

Vocabulary Preview

culture

language

tradition

artifact

festival

Circle examples of these words in the picture.

CULTURE FESTIVAL

custom

holiday

hero

veteran

landmark

Culture Is Our Way of Life

Different families eat different foods.

Aloha

Ciao

Hola

Jambo!

Yiasou

Every language has its own way to say hello.

Culture is a way of life. Culture includes our family, friends, and our community. It includes the foods we eat, the clothing we wear, and the places we live. Language, music, and religion are part of culture, too.

Our Language

Bonjour! (bohn ZHOR) This is what children in France say when they greet a friend. It means "hello." People all around the world have different ways of saying the same thing. **Language** uses spoken and written words to communicate ideas and feelings. Greetings are part of every culture, no matter where you live!

1. ◉ **Main Idea and Details**
   Underline one way we greet each other in American culture.

Draw a food that you like to eat.

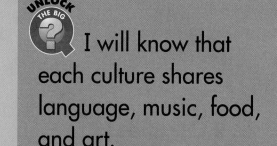
Vocabulary

culture   tradition
language   artifact

Our Music

Music can make us feel happy. Music is a part of every culture. It is something people both young and old can enjoy. We hum, sing, clap our hands, and dance.

Every culture makes its own music. Different kinds of instruments are used to produce special sounds.

Many children learn how to play instruments from their parents or grandparents. When children grow up, they teach their own children how to play their culture's music. This is called a tradition. A **tradition** is something that is passed down over time.

2. Write the name of a song you like to sing.

Calypso is a kind of music played on drums, rattles, and guitars in the West Indies.

Passing Down Traditions

People can pass down traditions through artifacts. An **artifact** is an object that was made long ago.

The Pueblo have been making pottery for hundreds of years. You can see some Pueblo designs on the pots in the photographs. Today, the Pueblo still make pottery using designs from the past.

Weaving cloth is a tradition for the Navajo (nah vah HOH) people. Colorful designs are weaved into blankets, rugs, and clothing. The Navajo use a loom, or a machine that helps keep cloth together, to make the designs.

Navajo children learn how to weave from their parents and grandparents. The woman in the photograph is learning to weave from her mother.

3. **Write** one way Pueblo pottery and Navajo weaving are alike.

_____

_____

_____

Got it?

4. ◉ **Compare and Contrast** How is one culture you have read about like your culture?

_____

_____

_____

_____

5. ? **What is a tradition that you share with your family?**

my **Story Ideas**

_____

_____

_____

_____

■ **Stop!** I need help with _____

▶ **Go!** Now I know _____

Cultures in Our Country

Envision It!

Families in the United States celebrate Thanksgiving.

People from many parts of the world come to the United States to live. They bring their cultures with them. All of these cultures make up American culture.

Albuquerque, New Mexico

Long ago, France tried to occupy part of Mexico. On May 5, 1862, a small Mexican army fought a big French army at the Battle of Puebla. The Mexican army won the battle.

Every year people in Albuquerque have a **festival,** or celebration, to remember the bravery of the Mexican army. It is called Cinco de Mayo, which means May 5th. Mariachi (mahr ee AH chee) bands play music. Dancers wear colorful costumes.

1. **Underline** one thing you might see at a Cinco de Mayo celebration.

People wear colorful costumes on Cinco de Mayo.

Write what this photograph tells you about the United States.

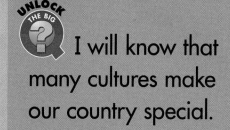
Vocabulary

festival

custom

New Orleans, Louisiana

Long ago, people from different cultures settled in New Orleans. They brought music with them from Africa, France, Spain, Ireland, and Germany. African American songs mixed with other kinds of music to become jazz.

Jazz is a big part of community life in New Orleans. It is played at baseball games, dances, and funerals. This tradition continues today. Every spring, people visit New Orleans to attend Mardi Gras. This celebration begins with a parade. Jazz musicians march down the streets while people clap and cheer!

2. **Main Idea and Details**
   Underline how jazz is part of community life in New Orleans.

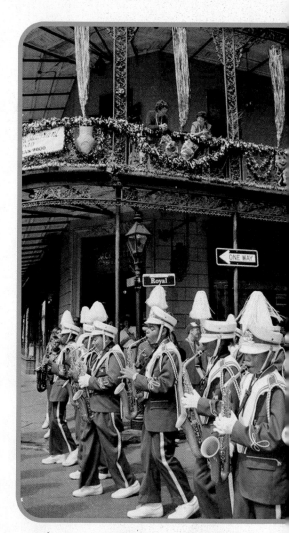

This is a Mardi Gras parade in New Orleans.

San Francisco, California

Many Chinese Americans in San Francisco live in Chinatown. In this neighborhood children speak both English and Chinese. Shop and street signs are written in both languages, too.

Each January or February, people celebrate the Chinese New Year. People from all over San Francisco go to the Chinese New Year parade. The parade blends American culture with Chinese culture. Marching bands play music. People dress in colorful costumes. A special dragon is carried down the street by more than 100 people!

Chinese New Year Parade

Before the celebration, it is a custom to clean your home for good luck. A **custom** is a special way that a group does something. It is also a custom to have a family dinner and give oranges as gifts.

3. **Underline** two Chinese New Year customs.

Chinatown, San Francisco

4.  **Compare and Contrast** How are the cultures of San Antonio and New Orleans alike and different?

_____

_____

_____

_____

_____

5. **What is a cultural celebration that your community shares?**

my Story Ideas

_____

_____

🔲 **Stop!** I need help with _____

▶ **Go!** Now I know _____

Compare and Contrast

When we compare, we find out how two things are alike. When we contrast, we find out how they are different. Look at the paragraphs about soccer and rugby. Details that show how they are alike are underlined. Details that show how they are different are circled.

Many children in the United States play soccer. Soccer is a sport that is played by (kicking a ball) and moving it. Soccer players run a lot. Players kick the ball into the goal to score a point.

Many children in New Zealand play rugby. Rugby is a sport that is played by (holding a ball) and moving it. Rugby players run a lot. When players get to the end of the field, they score points.

Read the paragraphs about cricket and baseball.

> Cricket is a sport played with a bat and a ball. Each team has eleven players on it. A game can last for several days.
>
> Baseball is a sport played with a bat and a ball. Each team has nine players on it. Some baseball games can last four hours.

1. **Write** one way that cricket and baseball are alike.

_____

_____

_____

2. **Write** one way that cricket and baseball are different.

_____

_____

_____

What We Celebrate

Envision It!

July						
SUN	MON	TUE	WED	THU	FRI	SAT
					1	2
3	4	5	6	7	8	9
10	11	12	13	14	15	16
17	18	19	20	21	22	23
24	25	26	27	28	29	30
31						

Look at the month of July.

A **holiday** is a special day. On national holidays, we remember important people and events from our country's past.

A Nation Is Born

Long ago, people in our country lived in 13 colonies. A **colony** is a place that is ruled by a country far away. England ruled the American colonies. People in the colonies did not think England's laws were fair. They fought a war against England and won their freedom.

Every year we celebrate our country's freedom on Independence Day. We have parades and picnics. We watch fireworks. We celebrate because it is our country's birthday.

Americans celebrate Independence Day.

1. **Underline** ways to celebrate Independence Day.

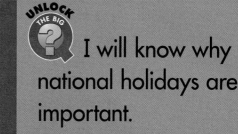
Vocabulary

holiday   hero
colony   veteran

Name a special day when we watch fireworks.

Remembering Our Heroes

A **hero** is someone who is remembered for bravery or good deeds. Our country has two national holidays to honor special heroes who protect our country. People march in parades and give speeches.

On Memorial Day, we remember United States citizens who died in war. Memorial Day is celebrated on the last Monday in May.

We honor veterans each November.

A **veteran** is someone who has served in the armed forces. Each November, Veterans Day honors the people who fought to keep our country free.

2. **Underline** the two holidays that honor special heroes in our country.

Thomas Jefferson

Remembering Government Leaders

Thomas Jefferson was the third president of the United States. Before he became the president he wrote the Declaration of Independence. Franklin Delano Roosevelt was an important leader during hard times. Americans liked him so much that he was elected president four times! We remember our presidents on Presidents' Day in February each year.

3. Write the name of another president.

_____

- - - - - - - - - - - - - - - - - - -

_____

Franklin Delano Roosevelt

Remembering Community Leaders

For a long time, African Americans were not treated fairly in the United States because of the color of their skin.

Dr. Martin Luther King, Jr. believed that all Americans, no matter the color of their skin, should be treated equally. Dr. King spoke out against unfair laws and helped to pass new ones.

Dr. King gave a famous speech in 1963. He shared his dream that one day all people would respect one another. We honor Dr. King and his dream on his birthday every January.

Dr. Martin Luther King, Jr.

4.  **Main Idea and Details** **Underline** one reason we honor Dr. Martin Luther King, Jr.

Got it?

5. ⊙ **Compare and Contrast** How are Memorial Day and Presidents' Day alike? How are they different?

_____

_____

_____

_____

6. ? How do you and your family celebrate holidays in your community?

 **my Story Ideas**

_____

_____

Stop! I need help with _____

_____

Go! Now I know _____

American Stories

Johnny has many seeds.

Johnny plants an apple seed.

Over time, American stories are shared by many people. Some stories have **facts,** or parts that are true. Some have parts that are **fiction,** or make-believe.

Folk Tales

A **folk tale** is a story from long ago about the lives of real people. Read these folk tales about three famous Americans.

Davy Crockett

Davy Crockett was born in a cabin in Tennessee in 1786. As a boy, he worked hard to buy a horse and became a great bear hunter. Davy grew up to be a soldier and a government leader.

1. ◉ **Main Idea and Details** **Underline** one fact about Davy Crockett.

Draw what you think will happen next.

Vocabulary

facts   folk tale
fiction   tall tale

Johnny Appleseed

Johnny Appleseed got his name because he carried sacks of apple seeds everywhere he went. His real name was John Chapman. Johnny planted many apple trees across the country. He wanted people to have enough food to eat.

2. **Underline** Johnny Appleseed's real name.

Betsy Ross

Betsy Ross made her living by sewing. One day in 1776, General George Washington, the leader of the American army, visited her. He asked Betsy to sew the first American flag. Betsy made a flag with 13 stars and stripes, one for each American colony.

3. **Underline** how Betsy Ross made her living.

Tall Tales

A **tall tale** is a story that starts off sounding true, but is mostly fiction. Read these tall tales and think about what parts are fiction.

Paul Bunyan

When Paul Bunyan was a baby, he was so big that he ate forty bowls of oatmeal each day! Paul had a giant blue ox, named Babe. He and Babe stomped around Minnesota as they played. Their footprints were huge. The holes filled up with rain and made 10,000 lakes!

Pecos Bill

Stories say that Pecos Bill was the best cowboy to ever live. He had a horse that no one else could ride. One day there was a tornado. Pecos Bill jumped on it. The tornado flattened forests. It rained so hard that the canyons washed away. He did not let go until the tornado died down to nothing. That is how people got the idea for rodeo riding. But instead of tornadoes, cowboys ride horses!

4. **Underline** part of each story that is fiction.

John Henry

There have been songs and books written about a railroad worker named John Henry. Some say that he was bigger and taller than any other man around. John Henry used his hammer to chip away at rock so that a big tunnel could be built. With a hammer in each hand, John Henry built the tunnel all by himself!

5. **Underline** part of the story that is fiction.

Got it?

6. ● **Compare and Contrast** How are folk tales and tall tales alike? How are they different?

_____

_____

_____

_____

7. ？ Which character in the stories do you like the best? Why?   **my Story Ideas**

_____

_____

_____

⬛ **Stop!** I need help with _____

▶ **Go!** Now I know _____

Two Cultures

Envision It!

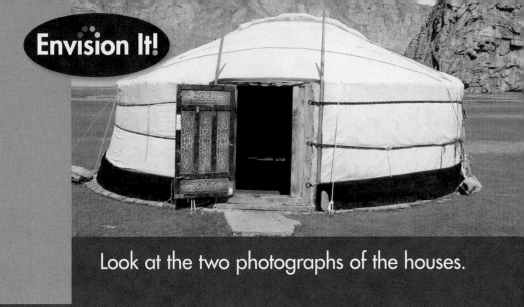

Look at the two photographs of the houses.

Cultures around the world meet the needs of their people in different ways. Read about the cultures in Mexico City and Beijing.

Culture in Mexico City

Mexico City is the capital of Mexico. There are parks and museums to visit. You can shop or eat in the city's many neighborhoods. Along the streets, there are people selling tasty food like tacos and tamales. At night, traditional music and dances are performed in the city.

The most popular sport in Mexico City is soccer. Many children play it after school and on weekends. Look at the picture of the boys playing soccer. Think about what it tells you about culture in Mexico City.

Vocabulary

ruins
landmark

Circle one thing that is alike.
Put an **X** on one thing that is different.

A long time ago, a group of people called the Aztecs lived in Mexico. Today, visitors from around the world visit Aztec **ruins,** or buildings that were lived in long ago.

Look at the picture of the Mexican flag. There is an eagle, a snake, and a cactus on the flag. These are symbols that were used by the Aztecs long ago. The color green on the flag stands for independence. Just like the United States, Mexico was once ruled by a far away country and fought to become free.

PACIFIC OCEAN   ATLANTIC OCEAN
Mexico City

The Mexican flag and a map that shows the location of Mexico City, Mexico

1. **Underline** one thing that you can do in Mexico.

Aztec ruins in Mexico

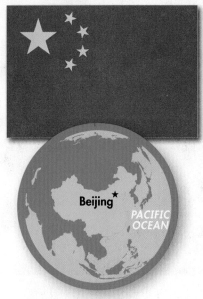

The Chinese flag and a map that shows the location of Beijing, China

Culture in Beijing

Beijing is the capital of China. It is a city that blends old and new. Many skyscrapers, or tall buildings, stand next to buildings from long ago. Many people in Beijing ride bikes. Riding is a popular form of transportation in the city.

Tiananmen Square is where celebrations and events have taken places for hundreds of years. Today, people fly kites. People do tai chi, a slow exercise to help you stay relaxed and healthy. People also stop to eat food that is sold in the square, like noodles, dumplings, and seafood.

Look at the picture of China's flag. The big star is a symbol of China. The small stars are symbols of the people of China.

Many people in Beijing ride bikes to get around.

Many visitors come to see the Great Wall of China. This **landmark,** or a structure that is important to a particular place, is more than 2,000 years old and thousands of miles long. Astronauts can see it from space!

2. ◎ **Main Idea and Detail** <u>Underline</u> three things you can do if you visit Beijing.

Got it?

3. ◎ **Compare and Contrast** How are Mexico City and Beijing alike? How are they different?

_____

_____

_____

_____

4. ❓ How is American culture like other cultures?

_____

_____

_____

⬛ **Stop!** I need help with _____

▶ **Go!** Now I know _____

Using Graphic Sources

A chart tells information in rows and columns. Columns run up and down. Rows run left and right.

Countries and Cultures			
Country	**Greeting**	**Landmark**	**Food**
China	Ni hao		
Mexico	Hola		
United States			

This chart is about cultures in different countries.
The columns tell what information you will learn.
The rows tell what countries the information is about.

1. Which three countries are named on the chart?

   _____

   _____

2. **Circle** a landmark found in China.

3. How do you greet someone in Chinese?

   _____

   _____

4. **Draw** a square around a food eaten in Mexico.

5. **Complete** the last row of the chart. **Write** or draw
   information about the United States in each column.

6. You want to add the capital of each country to this
   chart. Would you add a new row or a new column?

   _____

Lesson 1

1. (Circle) the photograph that shows an artifact.

Lesson 2

2. ◉ **Compare and Contrast Look** at the photographs. How are these celebrations alike? How are they different?

3. Draw a line to match each holiday name with a photograph.

Independence Day

Presidents' Day

Veterans Day

Dr. Martin Luther King, Jr. Day

4. Draw a picture of
your favorite folk tale.
Label your picture.

5. Fill in the bubble next to the correct answer.

A popular food in Mexico City is

Ⓐ pizza 　　 Ⓒ hot dogs

Ⓑ dumplings 　 Ⓓ tamales

6. Write what the photographs below tell you about culture in China and Mexico.

China

Mexico

 **Story Book**

Go online to write and illustrate your own **myStory Book** using the **myStory Ideas** from this chapter.

 **How is culture shared?**

In this chapter you have learned about cultures in different parts of the world.

© **W.2.6** Use digital tools for writing.

Think about your own culture. What customs, language, food, music, art, and sports do you share with your family and friends?

Draw a picture of your culture. **Write** a caption.

While you're online, check out the **myStory Current Events** area where you can create your own book on a topic that's in the news.

Our Nation Past and Present

How does life change throughout history?

Draw a picture of something in your community or family that has changed over time.

 # Begin With a Song

Living in America

by Henry Delaney

Sing to the tune of "Skip to My Lou."

Long ago they sailed the sea,
Traveled far with family.
Built homes in each colony,
They came to America.

Soon they wanted to be free,
Living independently.
Fighting for their liberty,
Living in America.

Vocabulary Preview

history

monument

explorer

settler

immigrant

Circle examples of these words in the picture.

pioneer

ancient

invention

civil rights

innovator

Life Then and Now

Envision It!

Look at the pictures above.

History is the story of the past. It tells about events that happened long ago. Each community and family has its own history. Each person has a history, too.

You Then and Now

What were you like in the past? You were very small when you were born. Over time, you grew and learned to walk and talk. When we talk about the past, we use the words *yesterday* and *then*.

What can you do today? You are in school, and you can read and write. When we talk about the present, we use the words *today* and *now*. *Tomorrow* tells about the future.

1. **Circle** words that tell about the past. **Underline** words that tell about the present.

Draw a picture of something that you did in the past.

UNLOCK THE BIG ?

I will know that people, families, and communities have a history.

Vocabulary
....
history   century
generation   monument

Families Then and Now

Events that happened in your family's past are your family history. You can ask a parent or guardian what life was like when they were your age. A family member from a different **generation,** or age group, can tell you how life has changed or stayed the same over time.

Long ago, families needed clothing, food, and a home. Today your family needs these things, too. However, there are differences between life then and now. Many families once grew their food in gardens. Today, most families buy food at the market. Families long ago played games, but they did not play them on a computer.

2. **Underline** two things that have changed in family life over time.

Communities Then and Now

Every person has a history. Every place has a history, too. People who have lived in your community for many years can tell about its history. Most communities begin with a small group of people called founders. When more people move to the community, the community begins to grow. The community may need to build more homes, schools, stores, or roads.

Communities Change

Sometimes a problem can cause a community to change. That happened to the people in the community of Enterprise, Alabama. About a **century,** or 100 years, ago, Enterprise was a rural community that grew a lot of cotton. Then, a bug called a boll weevil destroyed most of the cotton. The farmers knew they needed to grow something that the boll weevil would not eat.

Many farmers in the South had cotton crops that were destroyed by the boll weevil.

They discovered that peanuts grew well and the boll weevil did not eat peanuts. Today, many farmers in Enterprise still grow peanuts. The people in Enterprise built a monument in their community. A **monument** is a statue that honors a person or event. Solving the boll weevil problem was a big event in Enterprise's history!

3. ◎ **Draw Conclusions** <u>Underline</u> one reason people in Enterprise built a monument.

Got it?

4. ◎ **Fact and Opinion Write** one fact about a person who is part of your family history.

_____

_____

5. ? How has your family or community changed from the past to the present?

my Story Ideas

_____

_____

■ **Stop!** I need help with _____

▶ **Go!** Now I know _____

Reading a Timeline

A timeline shows the order in which events happened. You read a timeline from left to right, just like a sentence. The earliest event is on the left.

Look at the timeline below. It shows some famous events that happened in Florida's history. The captions tell more about the events shown in the photographs.

Events in Florida's History

1840   **1880**

1842
This picture of Florida's old state capitol building was created.

1887
The Hotel Ponce de León was built in St. Augustine.

Try it!

1. What does this timeline show?

   _____

   _____

   _____

2. Poet James Weldon Johnson was born in Jacksonville in 1871. **Circle** where you would add this to the timeline.

3. **Create** a timeline of important events in your life.

1920	1960	2000

1935
A hurricane struck the west coast of Florida on Labor Day.

1981
The Space Shuttle *Columbia* was launched.

Learning About the Past

Look at the photographs.

You can learn about the past by talking to people, reading books, and looking at objects. All of these are sources for learning about life long ago.

Primary Sources

A primary source is something that helps you learn about people, places, and events from the past. A **primary source** is a material that was written or made by someone who saw an event happen. Photographs, paintings, and drawings are some primary sources. They show what people looked like and what they wore in the past.

Journals, letters, and maps are also primary sources. A **journal,** or diary, is a daily record of thoughts and events in a person's life.

This journal tells about a journey across the United States.

UNLOCK THE BIG ?

I will know the difference between primary and secondary sources.

Vocabulary

primary source
journal
secondary source
biography

(circle) something that is the same in both pictures.
(M)ark an X on something that changed.

Secondary Sources

A secondary source also helps you learn about the past. However, a **secondary source** is written or made by someone who did not see an event happen. A **biography,** or book about another person's life, is a secondary source. This textbook is a secondary source, too!

People who study and write about history are called historians. Historians use many primary and secondary sources to learn and write about people and events of long ago. Each source gives clues about a person's life or an event that took place in the past.

1. ◎ **Main Idea and Details**
   <u>Underline</u> three sources you can use to learn about the past.

A biography is a secondary source.

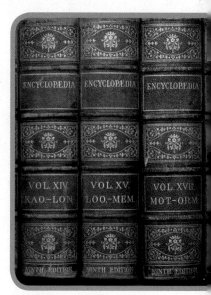

Encyclopedias are secondary sources.

Using Sources

The library in your school or community has many primary and secondary sources. Some of these are books, maps, newspapers, magazines, and encyclopedias. You can also find sources that give information about the past in museums. Museums contain sources called artifacts. An artifact is an object, like a coin or a stamp, that was made or used by people long ago.

You can also learn about history by using your computer and the Internet. If you type in key words about a topic, you will discover many Web sites about that topic. Many libraries and museums have their own Web sites where you can search for sources to learn about history.

2. Write some key words you would use to search for information about what children wore to school long ago.

_____

_____

_____

3. ◉ **Fact and Opinion** Is this statement a fact or an opinion? *Primary sources are better than secondary sources.* Which word is the clue?

_____

_____

4. ? **Write** one way you can learn about change over time by studying primary sources.

my Story Ideas

_____

_____

_____

_____

■ **Stop!** I need help with _____

▶ **Go!** Now I know _____

The First Americans

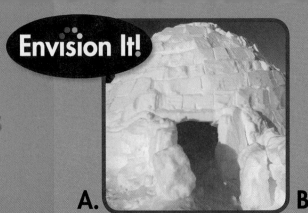

A.

B.

Look at the photographs of the different shelters.

The first people to live in America were American Indians, or **Native Americans.** Three Native American groups, the Plains, Pueblo, and Timucua (tee moo KWAH), lived in different regions. Each group used natural resources from their region for their food, clothes, and shelter.

Plains teepee

Plains people hunted buffalo for food, clothing, and shelter. They lived in teepees made of buffalo hides and wooden poles.

Pueblo people grew corn to eat, and cotton for clothes. They hunted deer and antelope. Pueblo homes were made from clay bricks.

Timucua people hunted bear and deer for food and clothes. Farmers planted corn, beans, and squash. Timucua homes were made from palm trees.

A. _____

B. _____

Write the material that was used to make each shelter.

1. ◎ **Main Idea and Details Look** at the map. **Write** "B" on the group that used buffalo for food, clothing, and shelter.

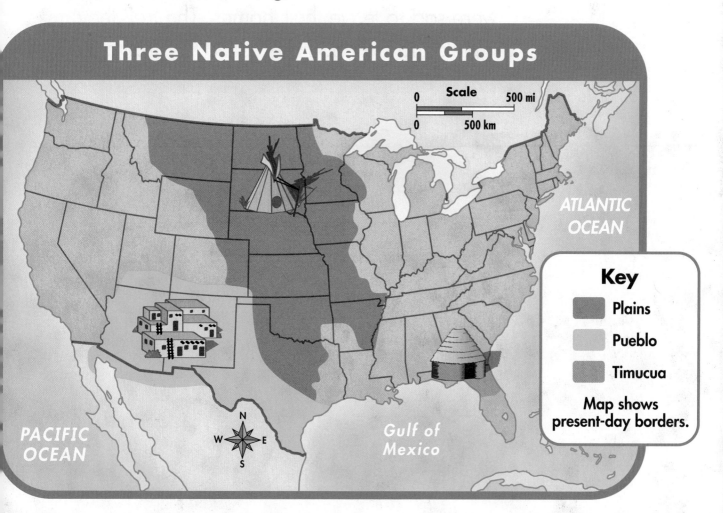

Three Native American Groups

Scale
0 _____ 500 mi
0 _____ 500 km

ATLANTIC OCEAN

PACIFIC OCEAN

Gulf of Mexico

N W E S

Key

Plains

Pueblo

Timucua

Map shows present-day borders.

Cherokee History

Long ago, Native Americans called the Cherokee lived where the states of Tennessee and Georgia are today. Their leader was called a chief. The Cherokee farmed corn, squash, beans, and sunflowers. They caught fish for food. They made some of their clothes from animal skins. They made their homes with branches and clay.

When people from Europe came to America, they fought the Cherokee for their land. The Cherokee were finally forced to move west to an area where the state of Oklahoma is today. They were sad to leave their homes. The trail they traveled to Oklahoma is called the Trail of Tears.

The Cherokee moved west along the Trail of Tears.

Wilma Mankiller was the first woman chief of the Cherokee. She worked with teachers to make Cherokee schools better. She made healthcare better for Cherokee people, too. In 1998, Wilma Mankiller received the Medal of Freedom from President Bill Clinton for her hard work.

2. **Underline** two things Wilma Mankiller did for Cherokee people.

Got it?

3. 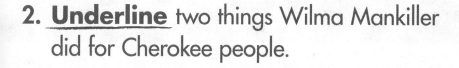 **Fact and Opinion Write** a fact about how Pueblo people used natural resources.

_____

_____

_____

4. **Write** one thing that changed for Cherokee people.

_____

_____

_____

_____

⬛ **Stop!** I need help with _____

_____

▶ **Go!** Now I know _____

America's Early Settlers

Envision It!

Write a label for each picture. Tell how people long ago might have used the items.

Long ago, explorers from Europe sailed to North America searching for gold and land. An **explorer** is a person who is the first to travel to a new place. **Settlers,** or people who make a home in a new land, followed the explorers.

Europeans in America

Spanish settlers built a colony in Florida called St. Augustine. A colony is a community ruled by a country far away. Shortly after, English settlers built the colony of Jamestown in Virginia. Native Americans often lost land when colonies were built.

Vocabulary

explorer
settler
Pilgrim

Life was hard for the early settlers. They did not have much food, and winters were very cold.

Another English colony was called Plymouth. It was in what is now Massachusetts. Plymouth was settled by people called the **Pilgrims.** The Pilgrims came because they wanted to practice their own religion. Native Americans helped the Pilgrims grow crops such as corn, squash, and beans. Every Thanksgiving we remember a feast the Pilgrims and Native Americans shared.

1. ◉ **Compare and Contrast Look** at the picture. (Circle) three ways life was different long ago.

Thirteen Colonies, One Country

Many colonists came to North America. In time, there were 13 English colonies. England made laws for the colonies and forced colonists to pay taxes. Many colonists grew unhappy. They wanted to be independent. They wanted to make their own laws.

John and Abigail Adams were colonists who spoke out against England's rule. John Adams said that the colonies should declare their freedom. Thomas Jefferson wrote a document called the Declaration of Independence. It said the people in the colonies wanted to be free. John Hancock was the first person to sign the Declaration of Independence.

England did not want the colonies to be free. England and the colonies fought a long war called the American Revolution.

Members of Congress from each colony signed the Declaration of Independence.

George Washington and soldiers of the American Revolution

George Washington led the army for the American colonists. In the end, the colonists won their freedom. The colonies became states. George Washington became the first president of our new country, called the United States of America.

2. **Underline** people who wanted freedom for the American colonies.

3. ◉ **Fact and Opinion** What was John Adams's opinion about England's rule?

_____

_____

4.  How was living in the colonies different from living in the United States today?

my Story Ideas

_____

_____

_____

_____

⬛ **Stop!** I need help with _____

▶ **Go!** Now I know _____

A Growing Nation

compass

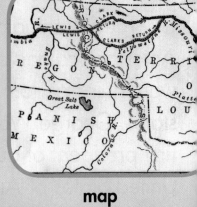

map

Look at the artifacts above.

As the United States grew, more and more immigrants came to live here. An **immigrant** is a person who moves from one country to another. The eastern United States was getting crowded. It was time to explore the West!

Moving West

Meriwether Lewis and William Clark set out from St. Louis, Missouri, to explore and map the West. Sacagawea (sak uh juh WEE uh), a Native American woman, helped them. Later, these maps helped people travel to new land.

A **pioneer** is a person who is the first to settle in a new place. Some pioneers moved to the West because they wanted a chance to own land, build homes, and start farms or businesses. Many families used covered wagons to travel on difficult trails that crossed through rivers and mountains.

Sacagawea

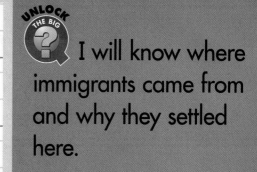

I will know where immigrants came from and why they settled here.

_____
_____
_____
_____
_____

Write how a compass and map could help explorers.

The map below shows some trails that explorers and pioneers used as they traveled to the West.

1. (Circle) places on the trails where it might have been difficult for pioneers to travel.

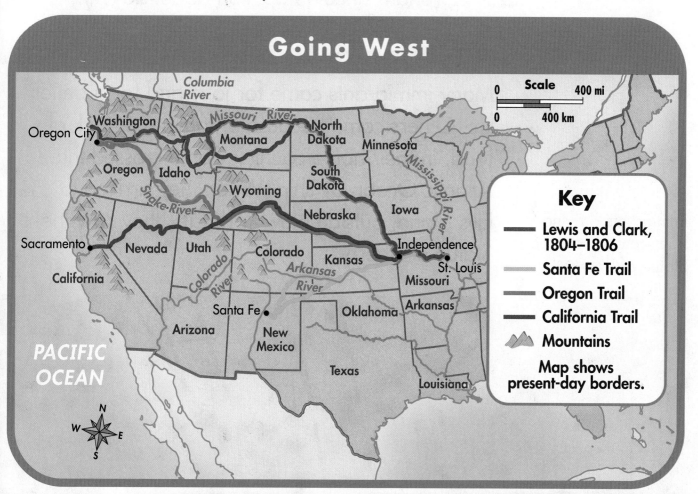

Going West

Key
— Lewis and Clark, 1804–1806
— Santa Fe Trail
— Oregon Trail
— California Trail
⛰ Mountains
Map shows present-day borders.

Not All Free

Many immigrants came to the United States for freedom. But African Americans were not free. They were brought here as slaves to work without pay. Harriet Tubman was one slave who escaped. Later, she came back to help others. She led about 300 people to freedom.

Many people thought slavery was wrong. Abraham Lincoln was one of them. He was the sixteenth President of the United States, and he worked hard to end slavery.

2. ◉ **Fact and Opinion** <u>Underline</u> Abraham Lincoln's opinion about slavery.

A Nation of Immigrants

Many immigrants came for jobs and for a better life. Others came because of famine, or lack of food, in their home country. Some crossed the Atlantic Ocean by ship. When they arrived at Ellis Island, outside New York City, they saw the Statue of Liberty.

Immigrants arriving from Europe saw the Statue of Liberty.

The Statue of Liberty has become a symbol of freedom for all Americans. Many immigrants still come to the United States in search of freedom.

3. **Underline** a reason that immigrants move to the United States today.

Got it?

4. ⊙ **Cause and Effect Write** an effect of immigration.

_____

_____

5. ❓ **List** two ways the United States has changed over time.

my Story Ideas

_____

_____

_____

_____

⬛ **Stop!** I need help with _____

▶ **Go!** Now I know _____

Technology Then and Now

Envision It!

Look at the photograph of a family traveling long ago.

Changes in technology over time make it easier for people to live and work.

Home Life Then and Now

People have always needed food, water, and clothing. In ancient times, people gathered plants and berries to eat. **Ancient** means a very long time ago. Later, Native Americans and colonists began to use horses and simple plows to plant seeds for food. People used wooden buckets to carry water from wells. They sewed their clothes by hand.

Today, farmers use tractors to plow fields quickly. Pipes bring fresh water into our homes. Sewing machines help us to make clothes faster. Modern technology makes life easier.

1. **Underline** two tools from long ago.

Colonists sewed clothes by hand.

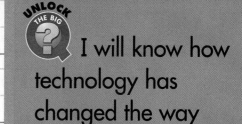
Vocabulary

ancient   telegraph

invention

Write about how you traveled to school today.

Transportation Then and Now

Long ago, horses were the fastest way to travel. There were no cars, trains, or planes. People wanted to travel more quickly. Some people came up with new ideas called inventions. An **invention** is something that is made for the first time. Karl Benz invented the car. Then, Henry Ford invented a way to make a lot of cars quickly. George Stephenson invented the train. And the Wright brothers invented the airplane.

A Wright brother flying over the beach at Kitty Hawk, North Carolina

2.  **Draw Conclusions Write** one way transportation inventions can be helpful.

Alexander Graham Bell made the first telephone call from New York to Chicago in 1892.

Thomas Edison made changes to the light bulb that helped it burn longer.

Communication Then and Now

In the past, it took a long time to communicate with others. It could take ten days for a letter to travel across the United States. Pony Express riders carried messages from Missouri to California by horse! Later, other inventions were used to send messages. Samuel Morse improved the **telegraph,** a way of sending coded messages over wires. In 1876, Alexander Graham Bell invented the telephone. For a long time, phones were connected by wires. Phones do not need wires to work today.

More Technology

If you had been born in 1850, your home would not have had electricity. The light in your home would have come from oil lamps and candles. Thomas Edison invented a new kind of light bulb in 1880. It could stay lit for a long time. Many people had electricity in their homes soon after that. Today, televisions, refrigerators, and computers all need electricity to work.

Thomas Edison also invented the record player. CDs, or compact discs, were made later. CDs are much smaller than records.

Today, people can play music on their computers and cell phones. What other changes in technology do you think you will see in your lifetime?

3. **Underline** inventions you use today.

Got it?

4. **Fact and Opinion** Is this sentence a fact or an opinion? *The telephone is the best invention.* Which word is a clue?

5. **Write** one way that transportation and communication have changed over time.

my Story Ideas

Stop! I need help with

Go! Now I know

Fact and Opinion

A fact is something that you can prove is true. An opinion is what someone thinks or believes.

Read the paragraph about Paul Revere.

Paul Revere

Many people believe that Paul Revere was the most important hero of the American Revolution. On the night of April 18, 1775, two lanterns were lit in the tower of North Church. It was the signal that the British were coming by sea. Paul Revere traveled from Boston to Lexington warning people so they could fight the British.

The sentence *Many people believe that Paul Revere was the most important hero of the American Revolution* is an opinion. The word *believe* tells you that this statement is an opinion about Paul Revere. Words like *feel* and *think* also tell you that a statement is an opinion. The other sentences in the paragraph are facts that can be proven.

1. **Read** the paragraph about Florence Nightingale.
Underline three facts about her life.

Florence Nightingale

Florence Nightingale was a leader of nurses. She helped care for soldiers during a war. She bought supplies. She worked day and night. She had a kind heart. After the war, she started the first school for nurses. Other nurses thought she was the best teacher. She wrote the first textbook for nurses.

2. **Write** a sentence from the paragraph that states an opinion.

American Heroes

Envision It!

Look at the photographs.

A hero is a person who makes a difference in the lives of others. There are many kinds of heroes. These American heroes made our country a better place for everyone to live.

A Wall of Heroes

John Adams

Adams was a Founding Father and our country's second president. He helped American colonists win independence.

Benjamin Franklin

Franklin was a Founding Father and a great inventor. He started the first public library in the United States.

Dolley Madison

Madison was the wife of our fourth president, James Madison. She helped make the White House a symbol of America.

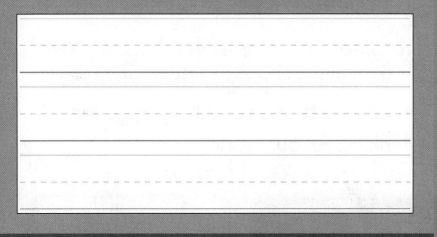

UNLOCK THE BIG ?

I will know about people who make a difference in the lives of others.

Vocabulary

civil rights
innovator

_____
_____
_____
_____
_____

Write how these people help others.

Heroes Make a Difference

Some heroes speak out for our country and its freedom. Other heroes speak out for the rights of people. These rights are called our **civil rights.**

Sojourner Truth

Sojourner Truth (SOH jur nur TROOTH) gave many speeches around the country for the rights of African Americans and women.

Cesar Chavez

Chavez spoke out for the rights of farm workers. He believed they should be treated fairly.

Harriet Beecher Stowe

Stowe wrote *Uncle Tom's Cabin.* This book helped people understand why slavery was wrong.

Some heroes have new ideas that help improve our lives. We call these people **innovators.** Other heroes take brave steps to change the way we think about our world.

Robert Fulton

Fulton built a steamboat with an engine. This steamboat could move people and goods faster than older boats.

Sequoyah

Sequoyah (si KWOI uh) invented an alphabet for the Cherokee language. It helped Cherokee people learn to read and write.

Henrietta King

King helped to improve the cattle ranching business. She gave money to build towns, businesses, and schools in Texas.

Amelia Earhart

Earhart was the first woman to fly alone across the Atlantic Ocean. She believed in women's rights.

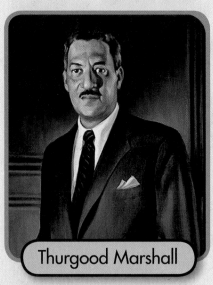

Thurgood Marshall

Marshall was the first African American Supreme Court judge. He also worked for civil rights.

John Herrington

Herrington is a Native American astronaut. He carried a Chickasaw flag into space with him.

1. ● **Main Idea and Details Draw** a picture of someone who is a hero to you.

2. ● **Fact and Opinion Write** your opinion of one of the American heroes you read about.

_____

- -

_____

3. ? **Think** about what life long ago was like for the people you read about. **Write** one way that life now is different from life long ago.

my Story Ideas

- -

_____

- -

_____

- -

■ **Stop!** I need help with _____

▶ **Go!** Now I know _____

Lesson 1

1. **Write** one reason that communities change over time.

_____

- -

_____

_____

- -

_____

Lesson 2

2. **Circle** the primary sources.

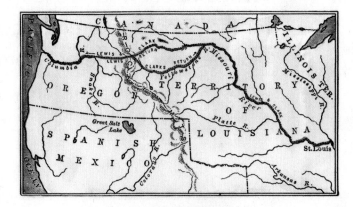

Lesson 3

3. Fill in the blank.

Native Americans used ______________________________

______________________ for their food, clothing, and shelter.

Lesson 4

4. Fill in the blanks.

Colonists fought for freedom from ______________________

They declared their freedom in a document called

____

Lesson 5

5. Fill in the bubble next to the correct answer.

Immigrants are people who

Ⓐ are the first to settle in a new place.

Ⓑ are ruled by another country.

Ⓒ move from one country to another.

6. Write how each invention changed people's lives.

_____

_____

_____

_____

_____

_____

_____

_____

_____

_____

Lesson 7

7. ◎**Fact and Opinion Read** each statement.
Write _O_ for Opinion, and _F_ for Fact.

___ Sequoyah invented the Cherokee alphabet.

___ Sojourner Truth worked the hardest for civil rights.

___ Robert Fulton built a steamboat with an engine.

my Story Book

Go online to write and illustrate your own **myStory Book** using the **myStory Ideas** from this chapter.

THE BIG ? How does life change throughout history?

In this chapter you have learned about history and the stories of people, places, and events of past times. You learned about how some people were not free and how others had to fight for freedom.

© **w.2.6** Use digital tools for writing.

Think about the freedoms you enjoy every day. **Draw** a picture showing what freedom means to you. **Write** a caption for your picture.

While you're online, check out the **myStory Current Events** area where you can create your own book on a topic that's in the news.

Atlas

The United States of America, Political

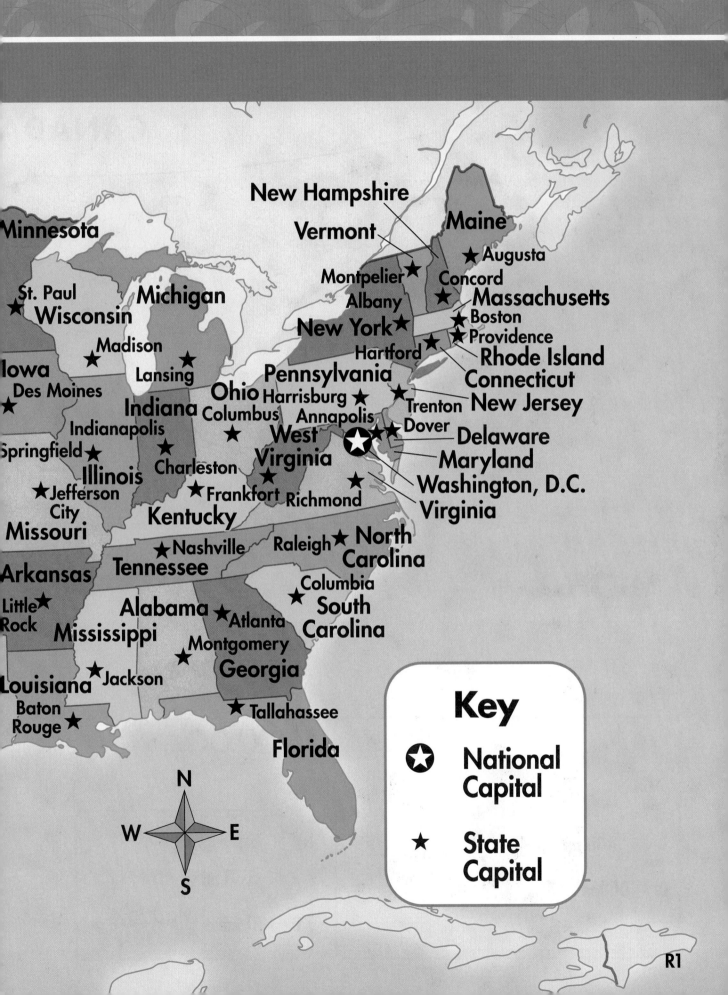

Minnesota

St. Paul ★

Wisconsin

Madison ★

Iowa

Des Moines ★

Springfield ★

Illinois

Jefferson City ★

Missouri

Arkansas

Little Rock ★

Louisiana

Baton Rouge ★

Michigan

Lansing ★

Indiana

Indianapolis ★

Jefferson ★

Kentucky

Nashville ★

Tennessee

Alabama

Mississippi

Jackson ★

Montgomery ★

Georgia

Tallahassee ★

Florida

New Hampshire

Vermont

Montpelier ★

Albany

New York ★

Hartford

Pennsylvania

Ohio Harrisburg ★

Columbus ★

Annapolis

West Virginia ★

Charleston ★

Frankfort ★

Richmond ★

Raleigh ★ North Carolina

Columbia ★ South Carolina

Atlanta ★

Maine

★ Augusta

Concord ★

Massachusetts

Boston ★

Providence ★

Rhode Island

Connecticut

Trenton ★ New Jersey

Dover ★

⬤ Delaware

Maryland

Washington, D.C.

Virginia

Key

⬤ National Capital

★ State Capital

N

W ✦ E

S

CANADA

▲ Mt. Rainier

Rocky Mountains

Gannett
Peak ▲

Great

▲ Mt. Elbert

Mt. Whitney ▲

Plains

PACIFIC
OCEAN

Rio Grande

MEXICO

Mt. McKinley
▲

0   400 mi

0   400 km

0   100 mi

0   100 km

Mauna ▲
Kea

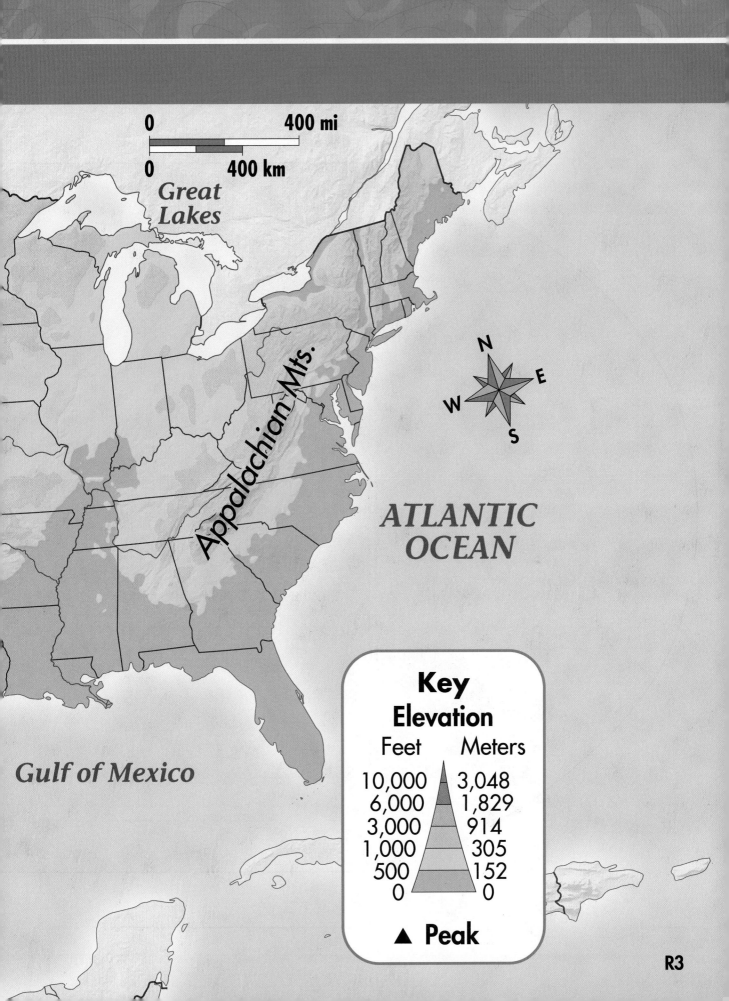

Great
Lakes

Appalachian Mts.

ATLANTIC
OCEAN

Gulf of Mexico

N
W E
S

Key
Elevation

Feet	Meters
10,000	3,048
6,000	1,829
3,000	914
1,000	305
500	152
0	0

▲ **Peak**

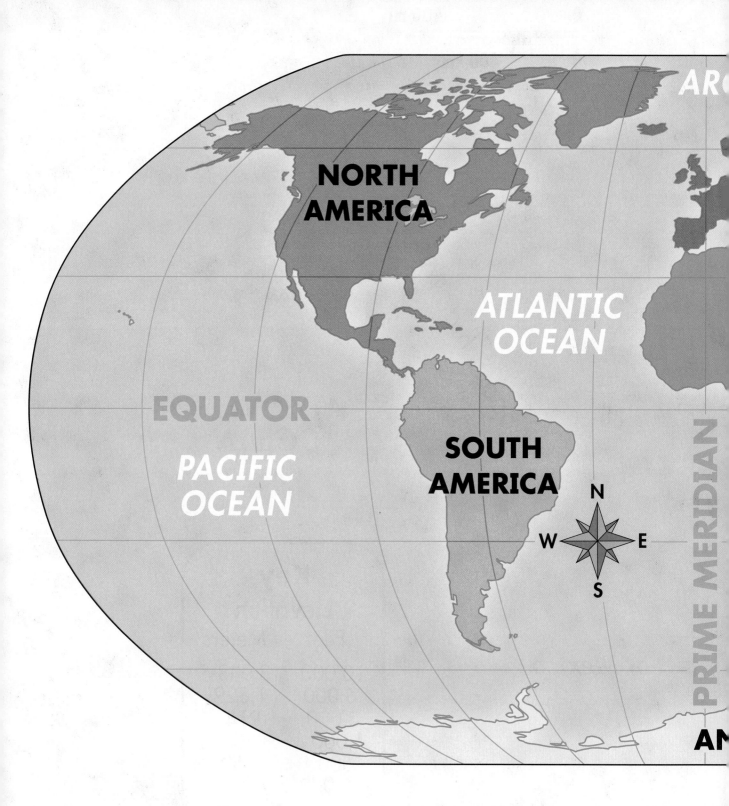

NORTH
AMERICA

ARC

ATLANTIC
OCEAN

EQUATOR

PACIFIC
OCEAN

SOUTH
AMERICA

PRIME MERIDIAN

AN

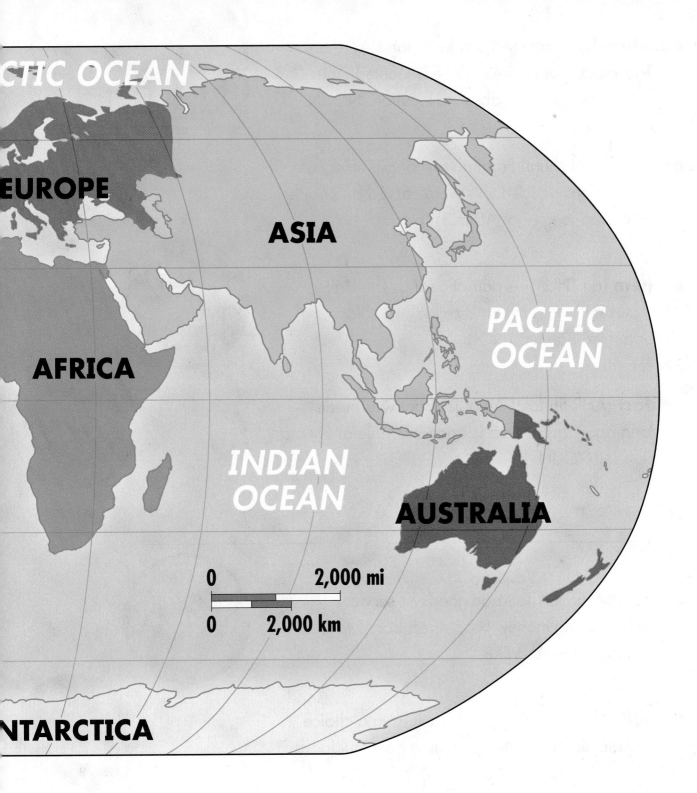

CTIC OCEAN

EUROPE

ASIA

AFRICA

PACIFIC
OCEAN

INDIAN
OCEAN

AUSTRALIA

| 0 | 2,000 mi |
| 0 | 2,000 km |

NTARCTICA

Glossary

A

absolute location (AB suh loot loh KAY shun) The exact spot where a place is located. Your home address is an **absolute location**. NOUN

ancient (AYN shunt) From a very long time ago. The **ancient** wooden toys were carved by people who lived long ago. ADJECTIVE

anthem (an THUM) A patriotic song. The United States national **anthem** is called "The Star Spangled Banner." NOUN

artifact (AHR tih fakt) An object that was made long ago. This **artifact** is good example of Pueblo pottery. NOUN

B

barter (BAHRT ur) To trade goods or services without using money. People can **barter** to get things they need. VERB

benefit (BEN uh fiht) A good result from a choice you make. One **benefit** of eating healthful foods is a healthy body. NOUN

biography (bye AH gruh fee) A book about a person's life. Jill read a **biography** about Thomas Jefferson. NOUN

borrow (BAHR oh) To use something now and pay it back later. If Tom does not have enough money, he can **borrow** some. VERB

C

cardinal direction (KAHR dnuhl duh REK shun) One of the four main directions on Earth. North is one of the four **cardinal directions**. NOUN

century (SENCH ur ee) One hundred years. About a **century** ago, people started to use cars instead of horses for transportation. NOUN

citizen (SIHT uh zuhn) A member of a community, state, and country. I am a **citizen** of the United States. NOUN

civil rights (SIHV uhl ryts) The rights of people. Cesar Chavez was a **civil rights** hero. NOUN

climate (KLYE muht) The weather a place has over a long time. Florida has a hot, wet **climate**. NOUN

colony (KAHL uh nee) A place that is ruled by a country far away. Each colony in America was ruled by England before the colonies won their independence. NOUN

communication (kuh myoo nuh KAY shun) The way people share ideas, thoughts, and information with each other. Telephones are used for communication. NOUN

community (kuh MYOO nuh tee) A place where people work, live, and play together. We live in a community. NOUN

Congress (KAHNG gruhs) The part of government that writes and votes on laws. Congress passed a law. NOUN

consequence (KAHN suh kwents) Something that happens as a result of an action. When Kayla did not do her home work, the consequence was that she missed recess. NOUN

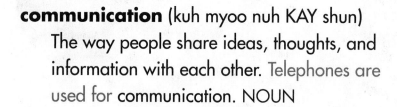

conserve (kuhn SURV) To protect the resources that we use. We need to conserve resources for our future. VERB

consumer (kuhn SOO muhr) A person who buys and uses goods. A consumer can buy goods at a store. NOUN

continent (KAHN tuh nent) One of the seven largest areas of land on Earth. Asia is one of Earth's continents. NOUN

cost (kawst) The price of something. The cost of the toy is five dollars. NOUN

council (KOUN suhl) A group of people chosen by citizens to make decisions or give advice to a community leader. The city council decided to build a new school. NOUN

court (kort) A part of our government where it is decided if someone has broken a law. The court judge decided that the woman did not break a law. NOUN

culture (KUHL chur) A way of life. It is part of our culture in the United States to celebrate Thanksgiving. NOUN

custom (KUHS tuhm) A special way a group does something. It is a **custom** on Chinese New Year to give oranges as gifts. NOUN

D

demand (dih MAND) The amount of something that people want. The **demand** for new computers is high. NOUN

E

environment (ihn VYE urn ment) The air, land, water, and life in a place. A city is an urban **environment**. NOUN

equator (ee KWAYT ur) An imaginary line that divides Earth in half. The **equator** divides Earth into The Northern and the Southern Hemispheres. NOUN

explorer (eks SPLAWR ur) A person who is the first to travel to a new place. Lewis and Clark were **explorers**. NOUN

F

fact (fakt) A part of a story that is true. It is a fact that George Washington was our first president. NOUN

festival (FES tuh vuhl) A celebration. We are going to eat delicious food at the Cinco de Mayo festival. NOUN

fiction (FIHK shun) Make-believe parts in a story. The story of Paul Bunyan is fiction. NOUN

folk tale (FOHLK tayl) A story from long ago that was first told aloud. Johnny Appleseed is a famous folk tale that many people tell. NOUN

freedom (FREED um) A citizen's right to choose what to do and say. Citizens have the freedom to speak up when they have something important to say. NOUN

G

generation (jen uh RAY shun) An age group. Children, parents, and grandparents come from three different generations. NOUN

geography (jee AHG ruh fee) The study of Earth. Jim looks at maps and globes in his **geography** class. NOUN

goods (goodz) Things that people make or grow. Many kinds of **goods** are sold in stores. NOUN

government (GUHV urn ment) A group of people who work together to run a city, a state, or a country. The **government** of the United States makes laws. NOUN

governor (GUHV uh nur) The leader of a state. The citizens of Florida voted for a new state governor. NOUN

grid map (grihd map) A map with lines that cross to make squares to tell the location of a place. The **grid map** helped us find the location of the Capitol Building. NOUN

H

hero (HEE roh) Someone who is remembered for bravery or good deeds. A firefighter who saves lives is a **hero**. NOUN

history (HIHS tuh ree) The story of the past. The history of a community tells how the community has changed over time. NOUN

holiday (HAHL uh day) A special day. Thanksgiving is a **holiday** when families in the United States have a big dinner. NOUN

I

immigrant (IHM ih gruhnt) A person who moves from one country to another. Ann's grandfather was an **immigrant** to the United States. NOUN

income (IHN kuhm) Money that people earn. Producers sell goods to earn an **income**. NOUN

independence (ihn duh PEN duhnts) Freedom from being ruled by someone else. America won its **independence** from England. NOUN

innovator (IHN uh vay tur) A person who has a new idea that helps to improve our lives. Robert Fulton was an **innovator** who built a steamboat. NOUN

intermediate direction (ihn tur MEED ee uht duh REK shun) One of the four directions in between the cardinal directions. Northwest is one of the four intermediate directions. NOUN

invention (ihn VEN shun) Something that is made for the first time. The computer is an invention that changed the way we live. NOUN

J

journal (JUHRN uhl) A daily record of thoughts and events in a person's life. Lewis and Clark wrote a journal while they explored the West. NOUN

L

landform (LAND form) The shape of Earth's land. A mountain is a large landform. NOUN

landmark (LAND mahrk) A structure that is important to a particular place. Mount Rushmore is a famous landmark in the United States. NOUN

language (LAN gwihj) Spoken words used to communicate ideas and feelings. Many people in the United States speak the English **language**. NOUN

law (law) A rule that everyone must follow. It is a law in many states that people wear seat belts while riding in a car. NOUN

loan (lohn) Money that someone borrows. He will need a **loan** to buy a home. NOUN

mayor (MAY uhr) The government leader in a town or city. The **mayor** spoke at the town meeting. NOUN

monument (MAHN yuh muhnt) A statue that honors a person, event, or idea. The Statue of Liberty is a **monument** that honors American freedom. NOUN

motto (MAHT oh) A saying that stands for an important idea. There is a **motto** on the Great Seal of the United States. NOUN

N

Native Americans (NAYT ihv   uh MAIR ih kunz) The first people to live in America, also called American Indians. Many Native Americans were forced to leave their land when the pioneers moved west. NOUN

natural resource (NATCH uh ruhl   REE sors) Something in nature that is ready for us to use. Trees are a **natural resource**. NOUN

needs (needz) Things we must have to live. Food, water, and air are **needs**. NOUN

nonrenewable (nahn ree NOO uh buhl) Cannot be replaced. Oil is a **nonrenewable** resource. ADJECTIVE

O

ocean (OH shun) One of the four largest bodies of water on Earth. The Atlantic **Ocean** is east of the United States. NOUN

opportunity cost (ahp ur TOO nuh tee kawst)
The thing you give up when you make a choice.
Between a computer and a bike, Carlos chose
the computer. The bike was the **opportunity cost.**
NOUN

P

physical map (FIHZ ih kuhl map) A map that
shows Earth's land and water. Anya found the
Rocky Mountains on a **physical map** of the
United States. NOUN

Pilgrim (PIHL gruhm) The people who settled an
English colony called Plymouth. The Pilgrims
were not prepared for the cold New England
weather. NOUN

pioneer (PYE uh neer) A person who settles in a
new place first. When the eastern part of the
United States got crowded, **pioneers** began to
settle the West. NOUN

political map (puh LIHT ih kuhl map) A map
that shows the location of places with imaginary
lines called boundary lines. A political map of
the United States shows the borders between
the states. NOUN

primary source (PRYE mer ee   sors) Material that was written or made by someone who saw an event happen. A photograph of an event is a primary source. NOUN

prime meridian (prym   muh RIHD ee uhn) An imaginary line that divides Earth in half. The prime meridian divides Earth into The Eastern and Western Hemispheres. NOUN

producer (proh DOO sur) A person who makes or grows a good. A farmer is a producer. NOUN

R

region (REE juhn) An area that shares special features. The Great Plains region of the United States has flat land. NOUN

relative location (REL uh tihv   loh KAY shun) The place where something is when compared to another thing. *Above* is a word that tells a relative location. NOUN

renewable (ree NOO uh buhl) Can be replaced. Wind is a renewable resource. ADJECTIVE

resource (REE sors) Something that is useful. Water is a **resource**. NOUN

respect (ree SPEKT) Concern for others. Good citizens show **respect** for each other. NOUN

responsible (ree SPAHN suh buhl) To take care of important things. Responsible citizens help clean up their communities. ADJECTIVE.

right (ryt) Something that people are free to do. Citizens have the **right** to go vote. NOUN

ruins (ROO uhnz) Buildings that were lived in long ago. Many people visit the Aztec **ruins** in Mexico. NOUN

rural (RUHR uhl) Having small towns and farms. Carolyn lives on a farm in a **rural** area. ADJECTIVE

S

save (sayv) To keep your money to use later. Kate will **save** her money to buy a bike. VERB

savings (SAYV ihngz) Income that you do not spend right away. In four weeks, Yoshi will use his savings to buy a game. NOUN

scarce (skairs) Not enough of something. We have to make choices when resources are scarce. ADJECTIVE

secondary source (SEK uhn dair ee   sors) Material that was written or made by someone who did not see an event happen. An encyclopedia is a secondary source. NOUN

service (SUHR vihs) A job a person does for you. A barber provides a service when he cuts your hair. NOUN

settler (SET luhr) A person who makes a home in a new land. European settlers started Plymouth Plantation. NOUN

skill (skihl) The ability to do something well. Learning how to read is an important skill. NOUN

specialize (SPESH uh lyz) To do one kind of thing very well. Some teachers specialize in teaching music. VERB

suburban (SUH bur buhn) Close to a city where people live. Port Washington is a **suburban** community near New York City. ADJECTIVE

supply (suh PLYE) How much there is of something. Boston has a large **supply** of fish. NOUN

Supreme Court (suh PREEM kort) The highest court in our country. The Supreme Court decided the law was not fair. NOUN

symbol (SIHM buhl) 1. An object that stands for something else. The bald eagle is a **symbol** of the United States. NOUN 2. A picture that stands for something real. She found the **symbol** for a mountain on the map. NOUN

T

tall tale (tawl tayl) A story that starts off sounding true, but is mostly fiction. The story of John Henry is a famous **tall tale**. NOUN

tax (taks) Money that is collected by the government from the citizens. Taxes are used to pay for schools. NOUN

technology (tek NAHL oh jee) The use of skills and tools. We use technology to make our work easier. NOUN

telegraph (TE leh graf) A way of sending messages over wires. The telegraph made it easier for people to communicate. NOUN

temperature (TEHM pur uh tyur) How hot or cold something is. The temperature outside is 64 degrees. NOUN

trade (trayd) To buy, sell, or exchange goods or services with someone else. People can use money to trade for things they need. VERB

tradition (truh DIHSH uhn) Something that is passed down over time. It is a tradition in Brian's family to have a big dinner each Sunday. NOUN

transportation (trans por TAY shun) A way to move people and things from place to place. A car is one kind of transportation. NOUN

urban (ur BUHN) Made up of a city and the places around it. Jean lives in an **urban** area. ADJECTIVE

veteran (VET uh ruhn) Someone who has served in the armed forces. Mr. Lee is a **veteran** of World War II. NOUN

vote (voht) To make a choice that can be counted. Citizens in the United States **vote** for the president. VERB

wants (wahnts) Things that we would like to have, but do not need to live. A toy and a bike are **wants**. NOUN

weather (WETH ur) What it is like outside at a certain time and place. Today's **weather** is sunny and warm. NOUN

Index

This index lists the pages on which topics appear in this book. Page numbers in bold type show you where to find definitions.

Credits

Illustrations

CVR1, 18, 28, 29, 43 Da Fanny; **CVR2, 12, 26, 47, 127** Laura Huliska-Beith; **2, 3, 4, 5** Robert Neubecker; **6** Modern Media Inc; **11, 140** Marion Billett; **14** Michele Noiset; **22** Viviana Garafoli; **30, 48** Carlos Aon; **34, 54, 55, 56, 74, 75** Paul Eric Roca; **53, 80, 112, 113** Nancy Cote; **58, 59, 160** Jenny Matheson; **62, 63** Ivanke & Lola; **68, 83** Dave Kirwin; **76** Christiane Engel; **84, 108** Mattia Cerato; **86, 87, 128** Aga Kowalska; **91** Noa; **144, 145, 146, 147, 159, 176, 177** Marsha Grey Carrington. **R6, R9, R23** Nancy Cote; **R8, R11, R17, R20, R21** Marsha Grey Carrington; **R8** Michele Noiset; **R9, R17, R20, R21** Paul Eric Roca; **R11** Kory Heinzen; **R11** Viviana Garafoli; **R12** Louise Ellis; **R15** Christiane Engel; **R17** Raul Allen; **R18** Aga Kowalska; **R21** Mattia Cerato; **R22** Robin Storesund.

Maps

XNR Productions, Inc.

Photographs

Every effort has been made to secure permission and provide appropriate credit for photographic material. The publisher deeply regrets any omission and pledges to correct errors called to its attention in subsequent editions.

Unless otherwise acknowledged, all photographs are the property of Pearson Education, Inc.

Photo locators denoted as follows: Top (T), Center (C), Bottom (B), Left (L), Right (R), Background (Bkgd)

Cover

CVR1 (BL) ©Nate A./Shutterstock, (CR) Ariel Skelley/Blend Images/Photolibrary Group, Inc., (TL) The Granger Collection, NY; **CVR2** (TR) Archive Images/Alamy Images, (TC) Danita Delimont/Alamy Images, (B) Dhoxax,2010/Shutterstock, (BL) haveseen/Shutterstock, (CC) Tom Grill/Corbis.

Front Matter

vi discpicture/Alamy; **vii** (CL) NASA/Corbis; **viii** Steve Skjold/Alamy; **ix** Vintage Images/Alamy Images

14 (BL) Purestock/Getty Images; **16** (B) ©Associated Press, (TL) Tom Grill/Corbis; **20** (BL) Steve Helber/©Associated Press; **21** (TL) Sean Justice/Corbis, (CR) Susan Biddle/ The Washington Post/Getty Images; **24** (TC) Lev Kropotov/ Shutterstock, (BL) OJO Images Ltd/Alamy, (TR) Stephen Bonk/ Shutterstock; **25** (BR) White/Photolibrary Group, Inc.; **27** (TR) Robert J. Beyers II/Shutterstock; **30** (BL) Yellow Dog Productions Inc./Getty Images; **31** (BR) Joe Sohm/The Image Works, Inc.; **32** (B) Steve Petteway/The Collection of the Supreme Court of the United States, (TL) Wally McNamee/ Corbis; **35** (CR) Jeff Greenberg/The Image Works, Inc.; **37** (TR) Haraz N. Ghanbari/©Associated Press; **38** (TR) Michael Newman/PhotoEdit, Inc.; **39** (BR) Susan Montgomery,2010/ Shutterstock; **40** (B) Pete Hoffman/Shutterstock; **41** (TR) Racheal Grazias,2010/Shutterstock; **43** (BR) Racheal Grazias,2010/ Shutterstock, (BC) White/Photolibrary Group, Inc., (TL) Yellow Dog Productions Inc./Getty Images; **50** (TR) Dhoxax,2010/ Shutterstock, (TC) Gemenacom,2010/Shutterstock, (BL) Richard Price/Getty Images; **51** (TC) bocky,2010/Shutterstock, (BC) Enshpil,2010/Shutterstock, (TL) Envision/Corbis, (CR) Tatjana Brila/Shutterstock; **52** (B) Alex Mares-Manton/Asia Images/Corbis; **54** (TC) Aprilphoto/Shutterstock, (TR) Elena Schweitzer,2009/Shutterstock; **55** (TL) ©DK Images, (TC) Hemera Technologies/PhotoObjects/Thinkstock; **58** (BL) Witold Skrypczak/Alamy Images; **59** (CR) Stuart O'Sullivan/The Image Bank/Getty Images; **60** (B) Hans L Bonnevier/Johner Images/Alamy Images; **61** (TR) Martin Heying/vario images GmbH & Co.KG/Alamy Images; **64** (TC) Hill Street Studios/ Blend Images/Corbis, (TR) Lisa F. Young,2010/Shutterstock, (BL) Patti McConville/Alamy Images; **65** (BR) JLP/Jose L. Pelaez/ Corbis; **66** (TL) Richard Lewisohn/Getty Images; **67** (TR) Tetra Images/Getty Images; **70** (BL) Bob Jacobson/Corbis, (TR) JLP/ Jose L. Pelaez/Corbis; **71** (CR) Joshua Roper/Alamy Images; **73** (TR) John Glover/Alamy Images; **74** (BL) discpicture/ Alamy; **79** (BL) Andersen Ross/Photolibrary Group, Inc., (BR) Ariel Skelley/Getty Images, (BC) christopher Pillitz/Alamy Images; **88** (TL) Hoberman Collection UK/Alamy Images; **90** (BL) istockphoto/Thinkstock, (TR) Thinkstock; **91** (TL) Andy Z/ Shutterstock; **96** (TR) Comstock/Jupiterimages/Thinkstock, (BL) NASA/Corbis; **97** (BR) Morgan Lane Photograph/Shutterstock; **100** (TR) Banana Stock/Photolibrary Group, Inc., (BL) Hemera/ Thinkstock; **101** (TL) Bill Stevenson/PhotoLibrary Group, Inc., (BR) iStockphoto/Thinkstock; **104** (BL) ©Masterfile Royalty-Free, (TR) Paul Tomlins/Flowerphotos/PhotoLibrary Group, Inc.; **105** (CR) Gavriel Jecan/Danita Delimont/Alamy Images, (BR) Mark Hamblin/Oxford Scientific (OSF)/PhotoLibrary Group, Inc., (TL) Rob Casey/Stone/Getty Images; **107** (TR) ©A. T. Willett/Alamy Images; **108** (TR) carroteater/Shutterstock; **110** (B) Ken Inness/Shutterstock, (TL) Patrick Eden/Alamy Images; **111** (TR) Tish1/Shutterstock; **114** (BL) ©DK Images, (TC) Anthony Cottrell/Shutterstock, (TR) Richard Drury/Getty Images; **115** (TL) Andersen Ross/Getty Images, (TC) Blend Images/Alamy; **117** (TR) Mike Flippo/Shutterstock; **118** (BL) 3d brained/Shutterstock, (TR) Andersen Ross/Blend Images/ Corbis, (TC) Stockbyte/Thinkstock; **120** (B) Jim Parkin/Alamy Images; **121** (TR) Sophia Paris/UN/MINUSTAH/Getty Images; **124** (CL) Jim Parkin/Alamy Images, (CR) Sophia Paris/UN/ MINUSTAH/Getty Images; **130** (TR) Kheng Guan Toh,2010/ Shutterstock, (TC) Stock Connection Blue/Alamy Images, (BL) Yadid Levy/Robert Harding Picture Library/AGE Fotostock; **131** (CR) Angelo Cavalli/SuperStock; **132** (TL, CL) ©DK Images, (B) ©Paul Chesley/Stone/Getty Images; **134** (TR) JGI/Blend Images/Corbis, (BL) Steve Skjold/Alamy Inc./SuperStock;